Back of the Hack

Back of the Hack
Growing up in the Liberties

By

Kathleen Clifford

ISBN 978-1-906353-40-7

First published in 2017
by
A. & A. Farmar Ltd
78 Ranelagh Village, Dublin 6, Ireland
Tel +353-1-496 3625 e-mail aafarmar@gmail.com

Cover photograph by R. S. Magowan
Cover design by David Cullen Designs
Designed and set by David Cullen Designs

Printed and bound by SprintPrint

In memory of Joe and Cathy, my mother and father,

— they did their best with what they had —

and of my sister Mary, who died young

Mullinahack or 'the Hack'

Part of the Liberties was called 'the Hack' by local people, shortened from 'Mullinahack' the name derived from the Irish 'Muileann an Caca' meaning 'dung mill or 'the mill of excrement'. Mullinahack was just outside the old city walls in the present-day area bounded by St Augustine Street, John Street and Oliver Bond flats. In previous centuries there were many mills in the locality, as well as whiskey distilleries, and numerous small businesses found a home here. Waste from the mills and animal and human excrement were taken from inside the city walls and dumped in Mullinahack causing a terrible smell.

Coming into the early and mid-twentieth century the mills and many of the businesses had gone and the name had been shortened by locals to 'The Hack'. Parts of its laneways and high walls were used by prostitutes and their customers. These unfortunate girls and women were at the lowest end of their profession. Homeless people huddled together in other parts and further down the darker side of society did its dealings.

As time went by the term 'back of the Hack' came to describe anyone whose luck had run out. They were said to be 'back of the Hack' when their life circumstances and finances were at their lowest ebb—hopeless cases.

Contents

Introduction 11

Joe, My Father 16

Cathy, My Mother 26

Little Creatures 39

The Blind Stew 43

Manna from Heaven 46

Annie 52

'Let 'em at it!' 56

Smoke Signals 58

Hotel Iveagh 66

Cures 72

Sheep's Head 74

Walks with my Father 80

The Boogie Man 85

Nancy and Dermo 90

Francis Street 94

School 99

Butch the Whippet 109

The Dispensary Doctor 111

Shopping and Pawning 117

On the Never-Never 122

Messages 126

The Seagull...130

Easter Eggs and Games.................133

The Bayno and other places 138

Mr Carbury Dies 143

Santa Claus...145

Joes Together 148

The Television Man..........................152

Tuggers and Toys for Rags............156

Hot Spot...161

Sheep's Wool and Fishing Rods ...164

Boileau & Boyd.................................170

Ever Ready 174

Bird's..177

Spot Dog Food...................................179

Aggie and Mags 182

My Sister Mary 186

Introduction

I was born in 1948, into the world of tenement life in the Dublin Liberties. Once-lovely old Georgian houses which had seen courtly gentlemen and their ladies socialising beneath their roofs, had been allowed to sink into disrepair and dilapidation. Gracious rooms were carved up by landlords into a maze of warrens and the poor of Dublin were the new inhabitants of these rooms.

When I was growing up nearly everyone around was poor. But there were different degrees of poverty. It was not unusual for some families to have ten or more children, and it wasn't easy for them but, as long as there was a regular wage coming in, they managed somehow.

My own parents struggled in poverty for all of their lives. My mother Cathy could neither read nor write, and my father had a bad limp and a deformed foot so for him getting work was always a problem. Sometimes he would earn a few bob from being a car park attendant, and other times he sold newspapers on street corners.

I remember sleeping on the floor in a house on Cork Street. It was my mother's friend's place and it was good of her to put us up. There were hostels for homeless men on the southside such as the Iveagh Hostel on Bride Road where you had to pay for your cubicle or the St Vincent de Paul Night Shelter up Back Lane. There were places on the north side too—the Mendicity and the Regina Coeli for women. But there were none that kept families together.

There was a place called the Sick and Indigent Roomkeepers' Society. It was situated in a laneway off Dame Street and near City Hall, at the side gate to Dublin Castle. There you would be interviewed as to your suitability for a room in one of the many tenement buildings around Dublin at that time. The room we got was in a building on Bridge Street. There was no water or electricity—we used candles and oil lamps. There was one cold tap in the yard below and one toilet which had to do for up to a hundred people including children. Also, the laneway leading in to the yard was open to the public and people came down to use the toilet. But at least we had a roof over our heads and it was a way of staying together as a family—my mother and father, my big sister Mary and me. The Roomkeepers arranged this and supplied the first rent.

The feeling I can remember most about our lives back then was as if we were living in a cave. Bigger rooms had been divided up and more people squeezed in and as a result some of the rooms had no windows. This of course fed in to the feeling of being cave dwellers. Large families were crammed into single rooms that had no water, no sanitation. Sometimes there were up to twenty people packed into such a room, with a bucket or chamber pot in the corner. Anything that needed to be done had to be done in the daylight hours as there was no electricity. Even so, to be fixed up with a room was no small thing as there were many homeless people like us about.

Everyone living there was in the same boat and there was a certain camaraderie amongst us. But once you went into your room you were an isolated unit. There seemed somehow to be a sad pretence that we were better off than we were. Sometimes we wouldn't have the rent money when the rent-man came around and it would be a case of hiding and not answering the door. We would huddle together and try to keep quiet until the rentman went away. 'Whisht,' my mother would say, 'Oul Siev is outside and he might be hidin' down the stairs.' I'm sure we weren't the only family who couldn't pay the rent every week, but it felt like we were.

With no running water or electricity it was hard to keep ourselves and the room clean. To get water we had to go down and fetch it up from a tap in the yard. All cooking had to be done on the open fire. If we needed to go to the toilet at night we squatted on a chamber pot or 'po' as we called it. We all understood the etiquette involved in this—we turned around the opposite way. It was too dangerous to empty the po at night as in the total darkness and the state of the rickety, partly rotten stairs, you could risk a bad fall—maybe resulting in broken bones. So in the morning one of us would carry it downstairs to empty it in the single toilet in the yard.

There was also an overall feeling of shame which was sometimes masked by humour. This was often black humour and the mothers were gruff with their children because they couldn't give them the things they asked for. So the abrupt manner often disguised a shame and desolation which if released could let the tears flow and there was no knowing when they would stop. If you met such women in the street you would think they were cheerful with their lot. Look behind the mask, however, and you would see pain and hopelessness.

I remember the women with babies, some of them wrapped inside their mothers' black shawls, and children everywhere. My family was considered unusual in these surroundings because there were only two children. All around us were families of anything from seven to fourteen children. Those women who were fruitful were continually pregnant and were old women before their time—as a result of continuous pregnancies, they often had missing teeth. To me as a child, it was unclear whether the women were mothers or grandmothers—if a woman of thirty was standing beside her mother of fifty, there would be little difference in appearance, apart from maybe a few more lines and wrinkles.

Some who had a dozen children or more had suffered five or six miscarriages as well. The Catholic Church forbade a woman to deny her husband his marital rights. Therefore she was expected to be available to her husband at any time he wished. There was a whole generation of children growing up who christened themselves 'The Guinness Babies'; some made a joke about it and said that Arthur Guinness had as much to do with their begetting as their natural father.

In my childhood, apart from school, there was very little communication with the outside world. So it was that verbal communication was very important in our lives. I remember many hours sitting in front of the fire or around the kitchen table listening to the adults talking, and in the case of my parents much of this was telling stories about their earlier lives. Sitting, listening to them talk, my mind conjured up images of people and places my father had known. This was not hard for me to imagine as many of the places he described still existed in Dublin. My mother's memories of her early life in Wexford, and later in Dublin, were vividly imprinted on my mind because there was such an overlay of emotion attaching to her words.

Sometimes as they talked, they forgot I was still there in the background—listening. To quote Robert Burns:

'A child's amang you takin notes.'

This is what I remember.

Joe, My Father

Joe was born in 1912. The Dublin he inhabited at that time was rife with TB. He, like his playmates, ran barefoot through the streets. 'Little gurriers' some called them but it was a case of survival. Going out, sack in hand, to the slack heaps, picking cinders to bring home for the fire. They begged opportunities to sell newspapers, run errands — anything to make a few bob. Nearly all the children came from big families, many of them inhabiting the tenements, living without sanitation or running water, all packed together in one room.

Joe and his friends Jemser and Jimmy spent most of their time on the streets. There were many horses and carts travelling the streets and consequently horse droppings along with dog droppings were strewn about. The numerous piggeries and abattoirs in Dublin attracted rats and these together with the resident rat population added to the general contamination. Usually the children only had to contend with stone bruises. These caused big white blisters on their feet, hard and sore with a little black in the centre. This caused terrible pain which was only relieved by sticking a needle in it and letting it all out. Occasionally, though, a cut on the foot would become infected from stepping in the shit and the wound became gangrenous. The gangrene quickly spread to the leg and then the only solution was amputation. They could be seen here and there throughout the city—little girl and boy amputees hobbling about on wooden crutches.

Joe's mother was a 'tugger'. Widowed at an early age and with five children, she had to find a way to support her family. Early every morning she went out with her cart to collect 'tugs'—old clothes and rags—from the big houses in the suburbs. This meant that Joe's sister Mary, at ten, was left to look after her two brothers and sister. Joe, at twelve, was the oldest boy and it was his job to go out and get money to help the family. Mary herself was a sickly child lacking energy, but she did her best for the family. Joe's brother Robbie was an epileptic and some days were worse than others when he would take fits three or four times. Mary on those occasions would take him back to their room and put him lying on his side on the bed they all shared. Sometimes it would be several hours before he came round. She watched over him and kept an eye on the spuds cooking on the open fire. Her other brother Frankie kept on at her to be allowed out with the other boys on the street. 'Ah, well,' she thought, 'he's nearly nine, he'll be able to look after himself.'

Sometimes Joe got lucky and heard about a toss school and where it was to take place. He begged the sham in charge to let him be lookout. Up to a shilling could be earned and besides, if he got on the right side of the winners, they might throw him a couple of coppers. There was excitement as the men gathered round and tossed their coins on the ground or against the wall. Card games, like toss schools, were illegal in public places and a lookout was required for these too. It was important to be in a position to run should the law show up. Joe would stand on a corner and keep a sharp eye out for the police. The agreed signal was to whistle if he saw the flash of blue or else shout 'Rozzers!' or 'Bluebottles!' Then the players would snatch up their money and scatter to the four winds, but later the sham made sure that Joe got his payment.

Another way of earning money was when one of the grannies sent him to the pub to fetch a gill of porter. It cost three pence for the porter and there was a ha'penny in it for him. Granny Whelan was a regular and sometimes she invited Joe in and let him warm himself by the fire. She had a poker heating in the fire and when it got red hot she dipped the hot end into her mug of porter. 'Ah,' she would say, 'that puts a good head on it and it puts iron in it too.'

Bewley's on Westmoreland Street was a good place to sell newspapers. Another boy would sometimes get to Joe's pitch before him and then there was no option but to fight for it. Joe was skinny but wiry and he often won the fight. When he didn't it was a case of finding another pitch, maybe in a not so busy street. From his vantage point, in between shouting 'Herald or Mail !' he watched the world go by.

At that time it was easy to distinguish between the

haves and have-nots. Their clothes for a start—poor women wore black shawls and often walked in a slightly bent-over fashion, as if apologising for their existence. Their faces had a pinched hopeless look—a 'what am I going to do to get food today' forlorn appearance. One of the big differences was footwear. Generally, the very poor were barefoot and in the winter they tended to scurry about in a hurry to get indoors. Sometimes Joe begged some sacking from tradesmen and this he fashioned into foot coverings and tied them about his feet.

Life wasn't so bad in the summer. At least then it wasn't so much of a hardship to be barefoot. Sometimes Joe and his friends would sit out on a step and talk with the neighbours. One of the neighbours was a Mr Brown. He liked listening to the children chatting and singing and one day he produced a couple of spoons. 'Would you like to learn how to play the spoons?' he asked them. Joe was eager to learn and all the children gathered round Mr Brown as he sat there humming and playing the spoons. Joe became adept at playing the spoons and soon he could do fancy moves like playing the back of his hand, or the side of his head.

Many happy hours were spent this way and it was around this time that he got the nickname 'Joeboy'. The 'boy' added on was meant to describe someone who was clever or crafty. He had noticed that when the men came out of the pubs they often rummaged in their pockets looking for money. Sometimes they dropped coins on the ground and Joe, Jemser and Jimmy would be waiting to dash in and scoop them up. If the men were really drunk the pickings could be richer—an odd half crown even! The boys knew that even if the men noticed them doing this, they would never, in their drunken state, be able to chase after them. Most of the money the boys made they handed up at home, keeping back a little of it to buy sweets or marbles.

There were dangers too on the streets—men who waited in laneways, trying to catch the boys' attention by rattling coins in their pockets, 'Come here, I want to show you something,' the gammy shee-sham would say. Then there was Mr Sheridan, a neighbour who lived in Joe's building. He always had his door open and a pot of stew cooking on the fire. He often invited girls in for a bowl of stew. There was one time when Joe's mother was passing the door and heard her daughter's voice. Unusually, the door was almost closed. She pushed in and saw Mary sitting there with Mr Sheridan. She called her out—'Come up outa that, I want you upstairs to help me with something.' Up in their room, Joe was surprised at how angry his mother was. 'You keep out of that oul fella's place, you hear me?' his mother shouted. His sister looked puzzled and annoyed as she had been enjoying the stew. 'But Mammy, Mr Sheridan was only bein' nice to me, he hugged me and everything.' 'Bein' nice, was he? I'm tellin' you now, never go into that place again, if I hear of you doin' that, I'll bate you

up and down them stairs.' They all got the message—
there was something gammy about Mr Sheridan.

Most of the people in Joe's world were decent and
just trying to live like everyone else. There were women
who would give you the last crust out of their mouths
and men who went out every day looking for work and
not caring what back-breaking work it was so long as it
earned them a few bob to feed their families. But there
were lousers too, who as the saying goes, would live in
your ear and sell the wax, would steal the coins from a
corpse's eyes. Gougers were even worse; it was said that
if they found a man dying in the street they would go
through his pockets and leave him there to die—would
literally gouge the teeth out of his head.

Then there were the lousers of officialdom. These
were people who took advantage of people's poverty
to cheat them. There were some people who owned
turf depots or coal yards who, when the poor person
produced their docket for free turf would give them
turf which had been doused with water to increase the
weight, or in the case of coal would throw in stones or
'clinkers' to weigh down the bags. They did this in the
full knowledge that the poor couldn't protest. When
they were sitting in front of the fire, getting 'diamonds'
on their legs from the heat, there was the hazard of
clinkers flying out, so that it would be necessary to have
the fire-guard up even though this diminished the heat
from the fire.

21

There was worry in the family about Joe's brother Robbie. The fits were getting worse and more frequent. His mother was out at work to feed the six of them and keep the roof over their heads. His sister Mary was looking thinner and paler by the day and it seemed that soon she would be unable to look after Robbie and the other three children. Joe's earnings from selling newspapers and his other moochings around were infrequent and although it contributed something to the family, it could not be counted on. Then everything seemed to happen together. Mary got sicker and was coughing up blood. She was fourteen when she died of TB. She was buried with all the other paupers in an anonymous grave in Glasnevin. Robbie was put into the 'Mad House' in Grangegorman. He wasn't the only epileptic there as at that time epilepsy was treated like other mental disorders.

There were now only three of the five children left at home. Joe's mother had to go out to earn, no matter what. His remaining sister was too young to be left by herself so it was up to his younger brother to mind her while Joe went out mooching. In his area he was thought of as a good prospect because he was capable of finding ways of getting money. It did no harm that he wasn't bad looking either.

The three lads—Joe, Jemser and Jimmy—ranged in age from twelve to fifteen and they were noticing the mots in their area. The girls would jeer as the boys went by. 'There ya are, Jemser, did ya get that black face from the coal or is there no soap in your place?'

Another girl would pipe up. 'Howaya Jimmy, did ya get that gunner eye from peepin' round the corner?' It would be Sheila's turn next. 'Look at Joeboy,' and she would jeer out the 'boy' part, 'are ya wearin' the rags your mammy collects?' These remarks were designed to get the boys to chase them and it worked. When the girls let themselves be caught, the boys might be rewarded with a snatched kiss. 'Who is your mot?' the boys asked each other later. 'Well, I have me eye on Goretti,' said Jimmy. 'I like Mags Daly,' said Jemser, and they looked at Joe. 'I like Sheila's hair,' he said as his face got red. So that settled it, Sheila was Joe's mot.

Now that he had a girlfriend, Joe felt energised to go out and earn more money. He still handed most of it up at home but he needed more to bring Sheila out. There were times when there was no money and they sat on the steps with the neighbours. Someone would start a sing-song, someone else played the harmonica and Joe would join in on the spoons. Later, as dusk came, people were encouraged to sing solo. Joe's party pieces were 'Beautiful Dreamer' and 'I Dreamt That I Dwelt in Marble Halls'. As he sang he really imagined himself in a better world, where he could stand upright, dressed in fine clothes and not a worry in the world. In his ordinary, everyday life, he thought of the day when he would be eighteen or twenty and he and Sheila could get married and get a room of their own.

He got the idea of going into town and maybe getting work cleaning windows in the posh squares whose houses had many windows. Others had thought of this already and he spent hours knocking at doors to be told by the housekeepers that they already had someone to do this work. He did get a few jobs, though, delivering fuel when the usual person was short-staffed. He also got the odd job cleaning windows when new people moved into a house and they had not yet made their domestic arrangements. It was while he was up cleaning a window that one of the rungs of the ladder gave way and he fell on the railings below. The railings penetrated through his foot and part of his leg. In the weeks following the doctors at the hospital discussed whether it would be best to amputate the leg or try to save it. In the end they saved the leg which now had a withered appearance. Joe was also left with a deformed foot with the toes all bunched together. It resembled an animal's hoof rather than a human foot.

It took him a while to get used to walking with his gammy leg. He felt ashamed to be seen in his neighbourhood, limping along. In the weeks he had been away Sheila had moved on. He didn't try to get back with her—after all, he had an affliction now. He had lost weight too and instead of looking wiry, he now looked skinny. He could no longer run or do any heavy manual work which was all his very limited education qualified him to do.

As time went on he watched as boys of his age in his neighbourhood got married and started families. He went past the usual age of eighteen to twenty-five when young men in his area got married. He would be well into his thirties before he found Cathy who became his wife.

Cathy, My Mother

Cathy, my mother, was born in 1923 in Gorey, County Wexford. When she was about three the family moved to Enniscorthy. It was to be a feature of her life—this constant moving. Because of this Cathy never settled in any of the many schools she attended and in some places she didn't attend school at all. The end result was that she grew up unable even to write her own name. In a couple of the schools she was made to stand up at the back of the classroom with a slate hung around her neck with the word amadán—'fool'—written on it.

Her mother was a stern, strict woman who was not without kindness, but she struggled to raise a family while coping with her husband's drinking and eventually her own. There were also her husband's bouts of malaria which were a consequence of his war experience with the British Army while serving abroad. His malaria attacks varied from relatively mild to days spent in bed struggling to banish memories of the war from his mind. On those days it was best to leave him alone because he couldn't abide company and in any case his ravings didn't make sense. There was the added caution needed in not letting people know he had been in the British Army. In those times he would be regarded by some as being something of a traitor.

Cathy remembered good times too when the family went into town to attend a fair or on market day when there would be a great atmosphere of excitement and anticipation. It started early in the morning when her father got ready the pony and cart to bring them into town. Sometimes they would have a jennet instead of a pony or horse and the jennet would be a bit more contrary than the other options. Their mode of transport depended very much on the financial situation at the time. If a jennet was used they could depend on it stopping and standing stock-still at least a couple of times on the journey and Cathy's father having to climb down to urge it on.

When they got into town Cathy and her sisters and brother were let off to explore the stalls and the trestle tables laden with a variety of goods. The children debated whether to spend their pennies on spinning tops, skipping ropes, balls or dolls, and if they bought one of these would they have enough to also buy toffee apples. These were serious matters and the children honed their haggling skills on those occasions. After eating their thick wedges of brown bread and drinking their buttermilk they felt refreshed and ready to enjoy the rest of the day. They hoped their father would keep well and not drink too much.

Sometimes Cathy went to visit her aunt who lived a couple of miles away. This aunt was unmarried and her house, as the saying goes, was like a doll's house in its neatness. Indeed, Aunt Mary had a collection of dolls representing the nations of the world. The dolls were displayed on a high shelf out of the reach of small hands. Cathy pleaded with her aunt to be allowed to hold even one of the dolls. She especially had her eye on a large baby doll which was dressed in fine lace and lay on a soft white wool shawl. Her pleadings were in vain for her aunt was not about to let her precious doll be handled by grubby little fingers. As they left the aunt's house Cathy's mother set her lips in a grim line and muttered; 'Them dolls will be there after her, when she's six foot under, so they will.'

The house was unusually silent at times when even the youngest child had learned to tip-toe around their father. Either he was in a delicate state because of his malaria, or he was recovering from the effects of alcohol. Their mother was often tense and nervous. Sometimes the children heard her muttering away to herself as she sat by the fire smoking her clay pipe. When she started drinking too, it made the situation worse.

Cathy could remember the time when her mother was happy, when she taught the girls how to make apple tarts and soda bread. It was a wonderful thing to watch her mother throw the flour on the table with a joyous flourish, roll out the pastry and cut small pieces of it for the girls to practice with. Then there was the delight of the aroma of fresh baking in the air and the anticipation of eating the delicious apple tart and soda bread liberally spread with fresh butter.

Her mother was great at story telling too. Many's the

time Cathy could remember her mother telling them stories of fairies and witches and doing the actions to go with the stories. On a dark winter's evening, while sitting around the fire, it was hard to distinguish between fantasy and reality and it could well be imagined that fairies danced outside and sometimes looked for an opportunity to swop a fairy child for a human one. In those times Cathy could remember her father looking happy too and even occasionally joining in the sing-songs and adding bits to the stories.

But all that seemed such a long time ago now that both her parents were drinking and it seemed to Cathy that maybe the fairies didn't restrict themselves to swopping children but changed grown-up people too. On pension day the parents went into town and after collecting the money they bought drink. The trouble was they didn't stop until a good deal of the money was gone. The pony had to find its own way home with the two of them lying down in the back of the cart.

An exciting time was when there was a wake in their neighbourhood. All the neighbours for miles around would go to the funeral Mass. Still more would show up for the wake. There would be, apart from the dead person's family and friends, others who professed closeness with the deceased which never existed in reality. In contrast with the family who often displayed a quiet dignity in their mourning, these professional funeral goers were the loudest in their keening and praising of the dead person's character. Even if the dead one hadn't a note in their head, it might be said that they could sing a sweet song—enough to charm the fairies or the birds out of the trees. Cathy, her friend Nan, and the other children thought all this was great craic but they were canny enough to show a serious face to the grown-ups. It wouldn't do to give the impression that they were enjoying themselves.

In the evening there was the gathering at the wake house. Bottles of porter would be provided and a couple of bottles of whiskey too. It was understood that the whiskey or poteen was for the men, but as the evening wore on some of the women would sneak a few drops of it into their mugs of porter. The men sat in one corner of the room and the women in another. Now and then someone would approach the coffin as it sat on the table in the middle of the room and toast the departed, sometimes letting a little alcohol drop on the lips of the dead. As Cathy and her friends watched the flicker from the flames of the turf fire fall on the corpse's face it seemed to them that they could see the lips moving. There was much squealing and poking of ribs as they frightened each other with the thought of the dead rising from the coffin. 'Maybe he'll dance a jig!' Nan screamed. 'Shush, he might hear you,' Cathy whispered. But they all fell about giggling at the thought of it.

The women sat in their corner with their black shawls wrapped around them and chatted. It was an opportunity to catch up on local news. The talk centred around upcoming christenings and who had left the parish and what the local shop was charging. Later the speculation was about why the Daly girl had gone off so suddenly and how Peggy Delaney got pregnant and she living on a farm miles from nowhere and her father and brothers the only men in her life. The women exchanged knowing looks as they smoked their clay pipes. It was frowned on for women to smoke in public but a wake was different and taking a sup and smoking were allowed to honour the dead.

The men clustered together and in the case of small farmers, talked about the going rate for livestock and how hard it was to make a living. The men in the company who were farm labourers kept quiet but later when they went outside to relieve themselves, they talked about how hard it was for them to feed a family on the money earned from casual farm work. But everyone cheered up later on as the alcohol did its work and someone produced a squeeze box and someone else a tin whistle and stories were told and songs were sung until well into the night and the next morning.

Cathy often walked in the fields with Nan and they talked about what it would be like to live somewhere else, to be in a city where there were many people, to stroll to a shop instead of having to walk four miles. As they lay in the grassy field they dreamed about what they might do when they were older. Cathy wanted to be a nurse and Nan a teacher. Cathy hid the fact that she couldn't read or write from everyone except Nan. She knew she could never be a nurse without having these skills but she hoped that someday soon her family would stay long enough in one place so that she could attend school regularly enough to learn. In the back of her mind she knew that simply learning how to read and write were not the only things she would need to become a nurse, there was the question of money too — money to train as a nurse was a far cry from her family's circumstances but she preferred to push these thoughts aside and dream instead.

As time went on, Cathy's sister Bridget got married to Bob, a farmer's son and they moved away. Her brother Michael, or Mick as he was better known, could only get seasonal casual work picking potatoes for the local farmers. This was back-breaking work and the pay was very small. His dream was to travel and see other parts of the world. As things were, if he stayed in Wexford he would never be able to do anything besides hard manual work and even that was only on a casual basis. Mick could only just about read and write so his options were limited. His father had been in the British Army so he determined to join up too. He was tired of being called a big buffer because he was tall and rangy and mainly unemployed. He was to see foreign parts all right but the things he saw during the Second World War left him with a damaged mind. He was captured by the Germans but he later said that they treated him well, giving him cigarettes and asking him what was he—an Irishman—doing fighting for the British?

When Cathy's father died suddenly it was a shock because even though he had been unwell for some time, still the suddenness of it took them all by surprise. Her mother's condition worsened and she became even more of a recluse. The younger children were sent to an orphanage. Then Cathy's mother decided they would move up to Dublin. Cathy was about seventeen at this time and she wondered why her mother wanted to make this move—they had no relations or friends in Dublin so there seemed no sense to it. When she asked her mother why they were doing this all she said was; 'That's for me to know and you to find out.'

When they arrived in Dublin they had nowhere to stay, so they walked around until they found a lodging house on the north side of the city. The landlady didn't seem to care whether they took the room or not, and a grubby little room it was too. The bedding was soiled and smelly and it was a noisy house with many comings and goings. After a couple of days Cathy noticed that the landlady sold drink to men who came to the lodging house. They often left with one of the girls who rented rooms there. Down the road was a 'kip house' and the men brought the girls there. Many times Cathy sat and cried while her mother slept. She felt overwhelmed by the noise and the smells. At least in the country there was space all around and people could go into a field to go to the toilet away from where they ate and slept, but here everyone was crammed together and there was only one toilet in the yard which was constantly overflowing.

Sometimes, when Cathy was going to the local shop she would bump into the girls as they left the house with their customers. Most of the girls were from the country and Cathy thought they looked exotic with their powdered faces and painted lips. Their clothes too were daring with their skirts only reaching to below the knee. Cathy felt dowdy in comparison, her clothes reached almost to the ankle. The men were interested, though, as Cathy was young and fresh and she looked different with her sallow skin, dark brown eyes and black hair. One of the girls gave her a half empty powder compact and a lipstick which was almost finished. She couldn't wait to get back to the room to try them out. When her mother saw her made-up face she got very angry; 'Take that raddle off your face, ya look like a hoor! If you don't stop talking to them girls and their fancy men, you'll hop against a knot one of these days, I'm tellin' ya'.' Her mother often came back with a bottle in a brown paper bag which she nursed to herself as if it were a baby. She sat there as the evening wore on muttering to herself and taking slugs from the bottle which was still wrapped in the bag.

Cathy got work as a domestic in one of the big

houses on Merrion Square. She had to leave early and walk there as there was no money for bus fare. She was expected not only to clean the house, but also to do the washing, ironing and polishing, and anything else the mistress of the house wanted done. The money paid was a pittance, scarcely enough to buy three or four days' food, but she knew there were women with large families who had been bargained down to even less because of their desperation to feed their families.

After a while Cathy made friends with some of the people who lived in the area, especially with Julia who came over from the south-side to visit her aunt. Julia, like most of the people Cathy knew, lived in a tenement room with her parents, six brothers and two sisters. Two of the brothers, John and Tom, hung around Julia and Cathy mainly because they had an eye for Cathy, but she considered them too young—Tom was fourteen and John sixteen. Cathy loved listening to their talking and bragging and pretending to be older than they were.

'I made one and six at the card school last night,' Tom said, 'an' I nearly threw a seven when I spotted the rozzers comin'.' 'Well, show us then,' Julia jibed, holding out her hand. 'I hid it,' he replied. John, not wanting to be outdone bragged about scutting on a horse and cart going into town. 'I had to jump off a couple of times when your man spotted me, but as soon as his head was turned I jumped on again.' 'Go way!' Julia and Cathy said in mock admiration. 'Yeah, an' then I scutted on a lorry.' He finished and waited as if for applause. 'If mam finds out you were scuttin' you'll get a right hiding,' Julia warned. The girls had a hard time keeping in the laughter.

Looking around her in the city, Cathy noticed the many raggedy, ill-nourished looking children. They often had flea bites and sores on their faces. There were so many of them, and she wondered how their parents could bear to see them like that. Many of the women seemed to have a baby every year. It was not thought to be a man's place to have much to do with the children, apart from finding work and putting food on the table. It was very unusual to see a man carrying a baby or pushing a pram in the street and if he did people would say of him that he was a mawfee man—a man with feminine traits. There were mawfee men who had large families, so their masculinity in the bedroom was not in question, it was just that they often had gentler natures and softer voices than was the norm. It was notable too that their wives were, more often than not, large dominant women.

After some time Cathy and her mother were in a bad way for money. Their landlady would not hear of waiting for her rent. And pointed out she could get more for the room by renting it to two or three girls. So they had to leave and after a couple of nights sleeping rough they got a place in the Regina Coeli Hostel for homeless women which was run by the Legion of Mary. Cathy's job was gone by now as she was too exhausted and dishevelled from sleeping rough to show up for work.

Some of the women staying at the hostel were prostitutes and some were like themselves—homeless because of varying circumstances. The rules in the hostel were strict; they had to be in early in the evening and leave early in the morning. Also, attending daily Mass was compulsory as well as regular prayers. Some of the women resented being preached at and the nuns who visited frequently were inclined to act holy and superior, at least in the women's eyes. 'Look at that beór,' one of the women remarked, 'look at the sour puss on her, an' she talkin' all the time about the joy of religion and the Catholic Church.' They called the visiting nuns magpies and the priest they called a sky pilot. 'Would ya look at your wan,' one woman said as a nun passed by, 'always talkin' about God and Jesus. Well, where was God when me children were taken and put into a Home? The nuns took them there so they did. Well, I'm tellin' ya, money is them nuns' God, so it is.' 'Stall the whids,' the woman beside her said, 'she might hear ya.' 'I don't give a flyin' fanny whether she hears me or not.'

Later on, Cathy and her mother managed to get a room on Townsend Street and it was a case of living from hand to mouth for a time. Things got a little better when Mick sent money to them but this was intermittent. There seemed no way of finding a way out of this poverty. Her mother was still drinking and seemed, on some days, not to care about anything.

When Cathy started going with my father she became pregnant and her mother threw her out. She spent her pregnancy sleeping rough on landings and streets with my father. They got married after she got pregnant.

My mother was starving and malnourished for nearly all of the pregnancy and the child came into the world undersized and with the pinched features that denote starvation. The baby was dead. The next child born was my sister Mary. She survived to the age of seventeen. Next came myself and less than two years later a boy, called Joseph after my father. When he was born my mother was alone in the room. This little soul died shortly after birth. That which had nourished him for nine months finally killed him. The child lay smothered beneath the after-birth.

Little Creatures

The very walls of our tenement room in Bridge Street teemed with life. The plaster on the walls was bound together with horsehair and was a breeding ground for the large brown bugs which crawled out and infested the beds and clothing. There was an awful smell from them and together with the outbreaks of the ordinary bedbugs they made life even more uncomfortable. Once a week there would be a cloud of white dust in the room as my mother fought the battle against the bugs with DDT insecticide powder. But no sooner did we rid ourselves of the infestation than a new lot would hatch out. I remember one brand of DDT was called Ovelle 666.

We could hear the rats scurrying about under the bare floorboards. They were especially active at night and there were many cracks and holes in the wooden boards through which they could come and go. Sometimes a large rat came out at night from a big hole in the floorboards and groomed itself in front of the fire. It sat there, whiskers quivering, brown body and sharp eyes alert for possible danger from us.

Like the rats, we slept together in the one space. There were times late at night when I looked across at the rat and it looked at me. I imagined it talking to me without making a sound—'I'm just trying to live, same as you,' it said. The rat had looked fatter and fatter and then one day it looked thin again. This made me curious and I quietly crept across to look down through the hole—I saw hairless pink and grey creatures squirming around below.

The mother rat arrived and I pulled back and held my breath as I watched her wrap the babies in pieces of paper. Later she assembled little bits of stale bread and other things I didn't recognise and wrapped them separately in paper and other materials. Then she lightly chewed the bundles and licked them until she was satisfied they were secured.

Now and then we heard about babies being bitten on the face by the rats during the night. What would happen would be that the baby would be put down to sleep for the night. The baby would burp and some milk would trickle down its face. The rats, being attracted by the smell of food, would lick the milk and in the process bite the baby's face. The rats slept a lot in the daytime. and it was then I brought my attention back to my family and the goings-on there.

There never seemed to be any financial planning by my parents for the week ahead or even the day ahead. I suppose it was hard to plan ahead without a regular income. Most of the rows they had were about money. My father, with his gammy leg, was not able for hard physical work, even if there was any available. So he mooched around, looking for casual work—car-parking, selling newspapers or herding cattle from the cattle mart to the abattoir for slaughter.

He would come in on such lucky days and throw the money down on the table. There would be maybe a half-crown or two, two-shilling pieces, some sixpences and thruppenny pieces. There would be no row that day and my mother would grab some money and sally forth with shopping bag to buy meat, potatoes and cabbage.

One day, I looked at the money still left on the table and thought—would it be a good idea to take some of that money and hide it away for the times when we really were hard up? So that is what I started to do—I wrapped some bigger coins in paper so that they wouldn't rattle and the smaller ones I rolled into little balls of newspaper. These I hid under the dresser, and waited with great anticipation for the next row. In my mind it had to be about money and we would have to be down to our last crust of bread. There they were again, shouting and cursing at each other; my father looking pathetic, my mother red-faced with anger.

With a flourish, I produced my collection. I really enjoyed watching the look on their faces. When the money was counted, it came to a few pounds—more than enough to see us through a few days. My father rubbed his hands and said 'There'll be wigs on the Green tonight.' My mother kept looking at me and then looking at the money. 'That child was in the world before.'

As for mother rat—for a good while she came up at night and groomed herself in front of the fire. Then one night I noticed her dragging her back leg behind her. After a while she no longer appeared and I hoped her babies were big enough to survive without her.

The Blind Stew

There were places in Dublin in the fifties and onwards where the poor and hungry could get free or cheap food. One of these was the Little Flower in Meath Street, also known as the Penny Dinners. When you went into the entrance beside St Catherine's Church there was a grotto to the Virgin Mary. At a side door, the nuns gave out the food. There was the option of eating there but my mother didn't like to eat in front of strangers. You could bring your own pot or tin to carry away the stew or other food given, and you were expected to pay a small amount of money. If you couldn't afford even that, the food was given to you anyway. Some called it 'the blind stew' because they said you'd go blind looking for the meat in it. If you didn't have a container, the nuns provided an empty sweet tin which had a handle for carrying. My mother brought a shopping bag to put the tin in so that the neighbours wouldn't see that we were relying on free food.

Another place was in Stanhope Street, but it was only for the desperate, as you had to queue up outside for the food. I remember standing in the hallway looking at the framed pictures of grim-faced nuns, among them Mother Mary Aikenhead. As a child I was very puzzled by this—who would call themselves that? I knew the spelling was wrong for 'aching head', but I couldn't fathom why a nun would choose a name like that. All sorts of things came to mind, like the wall advertisements for remedies for pain such as Beecham's Powders, Aspro, Mrs Cullen's Powders and the like. I had visions of Mother Mary Aikenhead sitting on her bed at night, with her head in her hands.

The food given out was nearly always stew, and sometimes in Stanhope Street it was so heavily salted as to be almost inedible. But as my mother said, 'Hunger is the best sauce.' Sometimes too, they gave out semolina, which I didn't much like as it was sticky and gloopy — with a dollop of jam on it, though, it wasn't too bad.

There was for me always a sense of shame and fear that the other children on the road would find out that my family went to these places. I could imagine their comments — 'Look at her now, who does she think she is, and her mother gettin' the free hand-outs.' I would never live it down. Of course, they were poor too, but there were different levels of poverty.

Yet another place we went to was Adam and Eve's Church on the quays. Besides the priests in the church there were another group of men called the Third Order of Brothers. I wasn't sure whether they were ordained priests or something like the Christian Brothers. Sometimes we would get a half-a-crown which was enough for two days' food. There was one occasion when my mother took me by the hand and we went down there. I watched as usual in the corridor while my mother went into the room to plead with the brother.

On this occasion though my mother came out looking pale and shaken. I tried to ask her what was wrong, but she refused to talk. However, at that time we were still in the tenement, living in one room so it was hard to keep secrets. I overheard her telling someone about it while I was supposed to be asleep.

'I was so afraid, he stood up and came around the desk and he put his hand on my chest, I couldn't believe he was doin' that and he a holy man and all. I tried to get away but he pushed me up against the wall and tried to put his hand under my skirt. He said, "Oh, come on now, don't be shy, sure don't you want money?" I pushed him away and got out of there. I tell ya I'd rather starve than let him up on me.'

And starve we did as it was two days later when my father got some work at the cattle mart. He got thirty shillings for the work and that saw us through another few days. In our world it seemed always to be either plenty or nothing, for if there was regular money coming in you could at least think a few days ahead. Maybe that was why my family made the most of the plentiful times as we knew the lean times were not far behind.

Manna from Heaven

Coming up to Christmas in 1954 we were far from feeling peace and goodwill. Another row was going on. It was the usual story — an argument over drink and money. My father shuffled around on his gammy leg, trying to make a few bob any way he could. But the lure of the pub and the company of the lads was sometimes too much for him. I suppose it was more enticing than going back to our damp, vermin-infested tenement room.

'Where were you up until now?' My mother asked him. Of course it was obvious from the brown porter stain around his lips where he'd been.

'Ah, Cathy, I was only out tryin' to make a few bob.'

'You were over in Sugrue's is more like it, drinkin' the money with that bunch of hoor-masters.'

My father rummaged in his pockets. 'Look, Cathy, here's two half-crowns, and there's a tanner there as well.' 'And how much did ya leave in the pub, tell me that.'

And it went on and on and we children only wished that it would stop, that our mother would stop shouting, and that our father didn't look so pitiful.

Of course, we didn't fully understand our mother's side of things. She'd been stuck in the room all day with nothing to give us but bread and dripping and going without herself. She'd long since pawned everything there was to pawn, and now even the free blankets we'd got from the St Vincent de Paul were in the pawn and we slept with old coats over us—all together in the one bed. We'd nothing to sit on either, as we'd burned our orange-box chairs to keep warm.

We'd been hearing in school all about Mary and Joseph and about how they couldn't find anywhere to stay and so Baby Jesus was born in a stable in some place called Bethlehem. We were enthralled to hear about how the three Wise Men, guided by a star, came to visit, bringing gifts of gold, frankincense and myrrh. We knew what gold was—wedding rings were made of gold, but we wondered what the other two things were. In the pictures we'd seen, the three Wise Men were holding the presents in little boxes, so we couldn't see what frankincense and myrrh looked like. We thought that maybe the frankincense was a present of perfume for Our Lady made by someone called Frank. The myrrh we couldn't fathom at all, though we did think it sounded like something you'd put in a stew—like parsley or thyme.

When we looked at the crib we thought it didn't look bad at all. There was plenty of hay for Mary and Joseph and the Baby Jesus to keep them warm, and they were wearing long cloak things that looked like blankets so there was no fear of them freezing to death anyway. And besides, hadn't they just got a present of a box of gold? All they had to do now was wait till morning and go down to the shops and buy all the food they wanted. We were delighted to think that Mary and Joseph and

Baby Jesus would not want for anything. And besides all that, we knew that the Virgin Mary had an orchard because some time before all this an angel appeared to her and blessed all her fruit.

My father's name was Joseph and my sister's name was Mary and I thought that maybe now that Christmas was coming, the fact that they were named after two such holy people would bring us luck, though I couldn't imagine anyone looking like the Three Wise Men would come knocking on our door. But you'd never know—strange things did happen. Didn't Mrs Brady downstairs get a baby and our mother told us that an angel brought it during the night. And then sometimes the angel changed his mind and took the baby back up to Heaven. Mrs Byrne, who lived two flights down, got a baby and when we asked where it was we were told it was gone to Heaven to be with the angels.

Two days later and the money had run out, and my father hadn't been able to get any more. After another row he went out again and my mother was crying. She took us children out and we walked for a long time away from where we lived. We were in an area where the people lived in houses. My mother knocked on doors and asked the people could they spare any food or money as we were starving. I suppose most of the people didn't have much themselves as they could only spare coppers, but my mother thanked them and hoped that God would bless them for their kindness.

We tried a priest's house and the housekeeper there gave us out a very large bone that still had some meat on it. It was what was left over from the priest's dinner. She said the priest was too busy to see us. We wanted to gnaw on it then and there as it smelled so lovely, but my mother wouldn't let us, saying that we'd make a show of ourselves eating in the street like that. We would have to wait until we got home.

Another time, when we were literally starving, my mother took us down to Rialto to try the houses there. It was like everywhere else—in some houses people slammed the door in our faces and in others they gave us a few coppers. There was one house, though, where an old woman answered the door and she brought us in. We didn't know where to be looking—the house had loads of lovely furniture and there were so many rooms too. I gazed in awe at all the photographs standing on the sideboard in their silver frames. On one side were family photos and on the other were framed photographs of the Royal family. I knew who they were from seeing them in newsreels in the Tivoli cinema. The old woman shook hands with my mother and gave her a ten shilling note. She told us her name was Mrs Black. She asked us to sit down and said she would make us tea.

We children sat very still as we were afraid to touch anything in case we left a mark on it. When she came back in she was carrying a large tray laden with sandwiches and all sorts of cakes. We couldn't believe our eyes. There was also a big delph tea-pot and cups with saucers to match. She talked to my mother as if she was a relative who had just dropped in, smiling kindly all the time, asking if there was enough milk in her tea and would she like a ham sandwich, or did she prefer cheese? Mrs Black noticed me staring at one of the photos of the Royal family and asked me did I know who it was. I wasn't sure but I whispered that I thought it was the Duke of Edinburgh. She smiled at me and seemed delighted and pressed a silver sixpence into my hand. She complimented my mother on how well behaved we were and how clever we were.

Mrs Black had lovely clean white hair, and strangely enough she didn't seem to have any wrinkles. Her skin looked as smooth as a baby's. The light from the window behind her cast a glow on her hair and lit it up like a halo. I was convinced by this time that she was an angel. When we were leaving she gave my mother a parcel of food and said she hoped that things would be better for us soon. Because she was an angel I felt sure that things would be better. I remember my mother smiling a lot on the way home. I hadn't seen her smiling in a long time and I knew it wasn't just because of the food and money, but also because of the way we'd been treated. We felt like human beings again.

Sure enough things did improve after that. The following day—two days before Christmas it was—a knock came to the door. Who was standing there only my Uncle Mick. We hadn't seen him in a couple of years as he had been away in England. At first I didn't recognise him because he was wearing a large woolly hat and his hair stuck out of the sides of it. I thought he looked like one of the Wise Men at first with his dark eyes and black hair, and he was wearing a long coat. But when he said 'How's she cuttin'?' I knew a Wise Man wouldn't say a thing like that.

This Christmas Mick was sober, and he had a bag with presents and food for us. He couldn't have been more welcome even if he had been one of the Wise Men. He gave my mother a few pound notes and my father went down to the tea merchants in Francis Street and got some empty tea chests. These were great to be used as a table and chairs and an extra one to put things in. That night we sat around a blazing fire with plenty to eat and I was delighted with my black doll, and my sister with her white one. There was no need for my father to go out in the cold and look for ways to get money. He and Uncle Mick had a few bottles of porter and Mick didn't drink too much this time. My mother was more than content with her tea and seeing that we all had enough to eat. It was a great Christmas and it seemed to me like a miracle the way Uncle Mick showed up when he did.

Annie

After a few years of us living in Bridge Street most of the tenements were judged unfit for human habitation and were demolished. My family were eventually housed in a Corporation flat on the third floor of a block of flats on a road off Patrick Street. Our flat was on the third floor. It had one bedroom, a scullery and a front room. There was no bath or shower but we had our own toilet located off the scullery and our own sink or trough with cold water tap. Around the corner on Bride Road the Guinness family had provided the Iveagh Baths where for a small fee you could use the baths and the swimming pool. Failing that, we had a large tin bath which hung on a hook in the scullery. So if we didn't have the fee for the baths, we could heat the water and have our weekly bath in that. The tin bath would be placed in front of the fire and my sister and I took turns as to who would get a wash first. All water had to be heated on the fire and so it wasn't practical to keep changing the water after each child. My mother would put bread soda in the water saying 'It'll soften the skin.' She would use a small pot to scoop water from the bath to rinse our hair and in it she would put an extra pinch of bread soda. 'That'll put a shine on it,' she said. You dried yourself on the previous week's clothes and got dressed in fresh clothes which, barring accidents, would have to do you until the next week's bath-time.

Down towards Church Street Bridge, just before the bridge, was The Brazen Head pub. At that time, it was a gathering place for prostitutes and their pimps, or 'banner men' as they were called locally. Our mothers would warn us not to go near the Brazen Head as the 'quare wans' would be there. It was hard to avoid contact with these women as there were many brothels nearby.

There was an area nearby, by a high wall, known locally as 'back of the hack'. This was a gathering place for prostitutes and their customers. Business here was on a standing-only basis and it was here that those unfortunates who had sunk to the lowest carried on their business.

One of them was Annie. Poor Annie was often too drunk to stand and so she ended up doing business on our back stairs.

The old prostitute would lie slumped on the concrete steps which led out to the communal yard at the back of our block of flats. White painted face and red painted lips. Without the aid of a mirror, the lipstick was smeared garishly on and outside her lips. The whole effect was to give her the appearance of a sad clown.

The next most noticeable thing was the smell. She would have been lying there all night, and the pool of urine beneath her probably helped to keep her warm; that and the cheap wine, or 'red biddy' as it was more commonly called. High in alcohol, low in quality, but it did its work in bringing oblivion.

There were six flats to be found once you entered this open hall door, each with their own stories, joys and despairs. We passed up and down as if Annie wasn't there. Indeed, from time to time she wasn't there. Then it was someone's turn to get out the bucket of water and Jeyes Fluid, open the back door and wash it all away.

We heard her speak, my sister and me, now and then. She had a country accent and try as we might to get past her without drawing her attention, sometimes she caught us. Clutching our clothing, she would lean in closer and tell us we were lovely children.

'Ye remind me of my own lovely daughters,' she would say. We stood there. The unwritten rule was that if you were caught, you had to listen—she was an adult after all.

'They took my own children away from me,' she would say.

'Yes, yes, they did. All because of that lyin' bastard, that husband of mine. Now they're down the country somewhere and he never lets me see them. Ah sure, that was years ago, they wouldn't know me now at all.'

As her story went on, her voice would keep rising higher until it ended in a wailing sob. My sister and me, we would take our opportunity and pull away, running two flights upstairs to our own flat. There we would sometimes find peace, sometimes drama and fighting, but at least we were 'respectable'.

Every so often as we went up and down the stairs, we would see Annie's customers scuttling away, heads down, eyes averted. 'Bye now, Annie,' they would say in that tone that implied they had tricked her in some way—maybe they had.

'Let 'em at it!'

There was a big hullabaloo and shouting coming from around the corner. We ran around to Bride Road to see what was happening. A large group of people were gathered there—mostly men. They were formed into a ring and were shouting with excitement. Being small we couldn't see what was going on so we snaked our way through the crowd and managed to hide ourselves partly behind the men at the front. Some looked around at us in a disapproving manner, but were soon distracted by the action inside the circle.

Two men were fighting in the middle of the crowd. They looked tired and staggered about a bit. The fight must have been going on for some time before we arrived as there was blood running down their faces, their knuckles too were bloody and one of them had a swollen lip. As one of the fighters staggered back into the crowd, he was pushed forward again. A skinny little man to the right of me shouted 'Go get him, what are ya waitin' for?' Other men threw punches in the air and called encouragement to the combatants.

The fighters had that 'boiled head' look of the habitual drinker and I guessed that they had probably been drinking in Sugrue's pub, or as the locals called it, Sugaroo's, on Bride Street when the fight broke out. This was not that unusual but what was unusual was the forming of a boxing ring on the street. Apparently these two men had a long standing grudge to work out. So it wasn't just an ordinary fight.

A large man stood in the circle keeping an eye on things. This was none other than 'Lugs' Brannigan, the policeman. 'Lugs' had gained his nickname because of the time he had spent in the boxing ring. He had large ears—'lugs', and a boxer's face to go with it. If one of the fighters was punching too low he stepped in and refereed the fight.

After some time there was only one man standing or more accurately, staggering and lurching about. 'Lugs' stepped forward and declared a winner. He helped the fallen man to his feet and made the two men shake hands. He then made each of them declare that this was the end of it, that things had been settled man to man and there would be no further aggression. They both nodded in agreement. Lugs' reasoning on this was because this was an old grudge the men might meet later on and maybe use knives or bottles and more serious injury could happen. Far better to settle it under supervision. 'Lugs' did referee in the National Boxing Stadium on the South Circular Road in later years and he was a boxer himself as part of the Garda team.

Smoke Signals

Woodbines and me go back a long way, so long, in fact, that I can remember when you could buy a pack of five. 'Wild Woodbines' they were called then. I used to wonder about that. I can tell you there was nothing particularly wild going on in my life at the time — unless you count my mother, and not forgetting my Uncle Mick. Or maybe it was because they were un-filtered. I think they were the cheapest cigarettes around at the time. Some called them coffin nails, because they had the reputation of giving you a really good cough. But old people at the time said they were made from the best of tobacco. But all I knew, when I was about ten, was that my mother and father smoked them, and this made it easy for me to pinch one now and then. I am sure my mother suspected this, but things came to a head one day, when I had got up early and sneaked into the toilet, which was located off the scullery. I had smoked about half the cigarette, when my mother started shouting, and pounding on the door.

'You took me last fag, you little yoke, come out and give it back!' I was terrified. My mother didn't mind so much that I was smoking, but it really annoyed her that I had taken her last cigarette, and she had no money to buy more. I decided to destroy the evidence, so I flushed the fag down the toilet. It was the worst possible thing to do. When she realised what I had done, my mother was madder than ever. When she finally got hold of me, the thumps I got were worse than at any other time. Yes, indeed, smoking really was bad for your health.

Patrick's Park was another great place for having a secret smoke. There was a shop there, opposite the back gates of the park, which sold loose cigarettes. You could get Woodbines, Players, or Gold Flake at two pence each. So, after school, two or three of us would buy our fags, and go across to the public toilets in the park to have our smoke. We hardly ever finished a whole cig, but would 'tap' it when half finished, and save it for later. We had it down to a fine art, because when the cigarette butt became really small, we would use a hair clip to hold it while we sucked the last 'drags' from it. We probably weren't even inhaling the smoke at the time, but a lot of the enjoyment came from the excitement of doing something forbidden.

Another place I associate with Woodbines is the Tivoli Cinema in Francis Street. We would go there for the 'penny rush'—the matinée on a Saturday or Sunday afternoon. After queuing outside for half an hour or so, the excitement would have built to a high pitch. When the doors opened we would all rush in, and take a place in the 'woodeners'—long wooden benches at the front part of the cinema. The middle and back part were cushioned seats, and were dearer than the 'woodeners'. We hardly ever paid much attention to the film on offer, as the noise was deafening, with constant shouts at the screen of 'Look behind ya mister, ya eejet ya!' or 'The chap is gonna get kilt!' When a romantic scene came on there was bedlam altogether. The shouting and whistling got louder, and the air was filled with missiles—gob-stoppers, peggy's legs, lucky-bag wrappers, and bull's eyes. There were also gobbets of spit coming down from the balcony, or 'golliers', as we called them.

Harry, the usher, was a big man, with a huge belly, and he considered himself not only the keeper of order, but also the moral guardian of all and sundry as well. He would roll down the aisle, torch playing over the benches, asking 'Who's makin' all that noise? Who's throwin' things around?' There was much tittering at this, and cries of 'Harry the blob!', or 'Harry the elephant!' This would madden him, but he wasn't able to tell where the voices were coming from in the midst of all that noise.

Harry's forte, though, aided and abetted by Con, the other usher, was to go up and down the aisles, and with the aid of a metal hand-held pump, squirt or spray, depending on how efficient the pumping mechanism was, disinfectant over us all. We might be sitting there, gazing in awe at Lana Turner or Lauren Bacall, doing their drama bit, when droplets of disinfectant would rain down on us. This was somewhat distracting, but it had a lovely smell.

I remember once, during a boring bit in the film, I sneaked out to the toilet to have a smoke. I must have smoked the cigarette too quickly, or inhaled too much smoke, because when I came out I felt dizzy, and staggered down the aisle trying to find my seat. Blundering about in the dark, I ran into Harry's belly. I bounced off it and lay there, flat on my back, Harry towering over me. He picked me up and shook me, his teeth grinding.

'You were smokin', weren't ya'?' 'No, honest, I wasn't.' 'You're tellin' lies now as well, I'll tell your mother on ya'.' The thought terrified me, much more than Harry did.

'Oh, please don't tell my mother!' A few seconds passed, during which I could imagine all sorts of dire consequences. 'All right then, I'll let you off this time, but don't let me catch you again'. 'I won't,' and I thought, 'no, you won't catch me again.'

I also remember the Tivoli because it was there that I first noticed that boys liked girls, and vice versa. It was the scene of my first romantic encounter. I was about eight at the time, and engrossed in the film—Flash Gordon I think it was. From out of the darkness a voice said—'I'll give you a Woodbine if you go with me.' I looked around in surprise. A chubby boy, smaller than me he was, was standing there, and even in the darkness his cheeks glowed red. I decided to ignore him. He coughed. 'I'll give you a picture of Elvis as well'. It was a tempting offer, and I considered it for a half minute or so, but seeing as I didn't know what 'going' with him involved, I decided not to accept. I shook my head. No, it would be less risky to get my own Woodbines, thanks very much.

Then there was my Uncle Mick. He was a regular Woodbine smoker too. My mother used to call him a big 'Baluba', because he was a tall, rangy man, with tanned skin, and wild black wavy hair, which no amount of combing or Brylcreem could tame. It shot back from his forehead in thick wiry waves, and my mother used to say 'you'd get sea-sick lookin' at it'. He also had large, brown, intense eyes, which stared at you in a peculiarly serious way, even when he was saying something quite ordinary like, 'Will you go to the shops for me?'

Anyway, Mick was very fond of cowboy and war films, and got really involved with the characters and the plot. This wouldn't have been so bad if he didn't go and have a few pints afterwards. The mixture of the two seemed to curdle his brain, and he really imagined he was Gary Cooper in High Noon, or John Wayne, or Randolph Scott. He would go out into the middle of the road, and stand there, cigarette dangling from his lip in true cowboy fashion, inviting every passing stranger to try him and see if he wasn't the fastest draw in the West. He would utter lines from whatever film he had seen, things like 'Meet me at Boot Hill', 'They died with their boots on', or 'Be on the next stage-coach headin' out of town'.

The result of this was that he was eventually barred from every pub for miles around, and had to go outside

Dublin town to get a drink. He was never known to harm anybody, but other customers didn't enjoy being asked to 'Step outside and get ready to draw', nor did they appreciate being told that he was 'the man with the Sheriff's Star, and he was going to clean up this town'.

Unfortunately, there was one time I remember, when Uncle Mick had gone to the pictures, and this time, instead of identifying with the cowboys in the plot, he decided to throw in his lot with the Indians. Even more unfortunately, in the film, the Indians, led by Crazy Horse, had burned the settlers out of their cabin, and Mick was inflamed with the excitement of it all. He arrived at our flat not only drunk, but he was 'Crazy Horse' as well.

My mother refused to answer the door, and we cowered there, listening to him shout lines from the film, and throwing in lines from other films as well. 'The good die young,' he announced ominously. There was quiet for a few minutes, and we thought he had gone away, but then we heard him making scratchy noises on the concrete outside the door. He had used up all the petrol in his lighter, smoking his Woodbines, but he had found a box with a few matches in it. It was when we saw smoke coming in under the door, that my mother decided that action was called for. It was time to send for the Cavalry. She stuck her head out the window — we lived on the third floor — and shouted for someone to get the police.

In the meantime, Mick was down on his hands and knees outside the door, blowing on the bits of paper, trying to keep the flames from going out. He was still in this position some minutes later, when the law arrived, in the shape of 'Lugs' Brannigan. 'Lugs' didn't believe in hauling people back to the Station, and wasting a lot of police time, if the situation could be dealt with there and then. Poor Mick was so engrossed in what he was doing that he was completely unaware, until he felt a huge hand grab him by the scruff of the neck and haul him upright. Mick was big, but 'Lugs' was bigger. He pulled Mick up, close to his face—'Threatenin' women and children, that's your strength, eh? How about takin' me on, what do you think of that notion?' Lugs always carried a pair of leather gloves in his hand, and he now used them to clatter Mick with. Mick looked terrified. We watched as he was strong-armed down the stairs. Then we rushed to the window to see what was happening next. We saw Mick being escorted to the top of the road, and then Lugs gave him a kick up the backside and sent him on his way.

My mother wouldn't allow Uncle Mick inside the flat for a full week after that. But then he arrived with a 'wrap-up'—meaty bones for boiling, wrapped up in newspaper, and my mother relented.

'You know,' she said, 'poor Mick wouldn't be as bad as he was, if he hadn't seen terrible things in foreign parts during the war.'

All the same, though, when, a few days later, I was passing by the Tivoli, and I saw that the upcoming attraction was Gunfight at the OK Corral, I thought I'd better go home and warn my mother. After all, we had already had a visitation from Crazy Horse, so we didn't want Wyatt Earp showing up as well. We were lucky though, for on Mick's next outing to the cinema, he went up to the Lyric in James's Street. There was a cowboy film on there, but Mick didn't realise until it was too late that the cowboy was Gene Autry, the singing cowboy. Mick was disappointed, but we were delighted. Things were quiet for a while after that.

Hotel Iveagh

We lived around the corner from the Iveagh Hostel for
men, and no matter which direction you were going —
whether it was up Bride Street, or down the cobbles of
Nicholas Street Hill, which led on to Patrick Street, you
could always see one of the inhabitants of the Iveagh
standing on a corner. When they hadn't even the few
pence necessary to gain admittance there, the next step
downward was Back Lane — the night shelter for homeless men run by the St Vincent de Paul. This was situated
across the road from the Iveagh. The doss-houses in our
general area ranged in quality from a reasonably decent
mattress on the floor, and not too many bed bugs, to the
cheapest where a rope was strung across the room and
people tried to sleep standing up, leaning on the rope.

Some of the men who stayed in the Iveagh did so
for only a short time. These were usually up from the
country, and when they had no luck finding work in
Dublin, they took the boat to England, hoping to find
work there. Very few ever went back home, for to do so
was to admit defeat. It was sad to see the hope fading in
their eyes, as week followed week, and the money running out with each passing day.

There were also the long-stay residents. These were
men who couldn't raise the money to either go to England or return home. In some cases, they became too
depressed and lost the will to strive to do anything

much at all. Side by side with these unfortunates, were the characters that were considered a bit odd, or downright mad. It is debatable which group was worse off, as people who are fully aware of how badly off they are would seem, on the face of it, to be capable of suffering more mental anguish. But who can say for sure? All I can say is that the men I remember most when a child stayed more vividly imprinted on my mind because they were unusual or colourful.

There was a man we named 'Flower' who usually occupied the spot on the corner of Bride Road and New Bride Street. He would stand there, a portly, dapper man, looking the perfect gentleman in his well-cut, though shabby suit. He sported a bowler hat, and in his hand he carried a black walking stick with a silver-coloured top on it. He always wore a flower in his lapel — hence his nickname — and the type of flower depended on what was growing at the time in nearby Patrick's Park. We didn't get much fun out of him though, as he always had about him a stately air, and no matter how much we gathered round and tried to 'draw him out', he refused to be baited.

He would just stand there, and look down on us with a superior expression and say things like — 'Good day to you', or 'Won't you be expected home for lunch soon?' We thought this was very funny, as we didn't have 'lunch', just dinner.

There was another man we called 'The Lump'

because he had a huge growth coming out of the side of his neck and resting partly on his shoulder, partly on his chest. As the years went by, the lump grew bigger. He would emerge from the Iveagh and stroll down the road to stand beside 'Flower' who occupied his usual spot on the corner. 'Flower' would look aggrieved at this incursion on his territory. After a series of coughs and 'Ahems', which didn't seem to get through to 'The Lump' who stood gazing straight ahead of him, 'Flower' would stride off looking thoroughly affronted. I suppose as far as 'The Lump' was concerned this was the whole object of the exercise.

There came a day when 'The Lump' was no longer to be seen on his usual corner. We wondered about this, and made up all sorts of fantastic stories about his disappearance. A couple of weeks later I overheard my mother talking about him to a neighbour.

'They opened him up, above in the hospital, and he didn't last no time after that.'

'They should have left that lump alone, sure what harm was it doin'? It's always the way, once they let the air at it, then the person is done for.'

'I know what you mean. The poor man, there he is now with no lump, but no life in him either, buried above in a pauper's grave in Glasnevin.'

Then there was the man called 'Ride your bike' who strolled around pushing his bike beside him. We never saw him astride the bike and would call out after him—

'Go on, mister, ride your bike, what are you waitin' for, is there a train comin' or wha'?' He would quicken his pace to get away from the taunting, running along beside his bike, and the wheels of his bike would make a whining noise as he hurried along.

Another variation on the 'Flower' theme was a man called 'Wallflower'. He would stand on a less favoured corner, the one looking down Patrick Street, only he didn't look down the street, but stood talking to the wall. He didn't talk to the wall every day, mind, just on those days when there was something in particular worrying him. Then he would hurry down the street, his hands jammed into his pockets, his head bent, peering at the ground, muttering to himself. When he arrived at that part of the wall which he found conducive to conversation, he would stand there talking and gesturing with his hands, and every now and then would become still—nodding his head and listening to what the wall had to say.

I remember one occasion when 'Wallflower' was having his usual conversation with the bricks and 'Flower' happened to be passing by, looking jaunty and twirling his cane. He stood for a moment regarding 'Wallflower' with a serious expression on his face.

Then he turned to me and tapping the side of his head, he said—'Poor soul, quite troubled, you know, he really should be getting treatment.'

'Where are you goin', Flower?' I asked him. 'Well, I

think I'll try the Gresham Hotel for a spot of lunch to-day. I was disappointed with the Shelbourne yesterday, not quite up to standard, you know.'

The most enduring memory I have is of the man called 'Clare', so called because that was his county of origin. I saw him often because he usually stood on the corner of Bride Road and Patrick Street, and my mother sent me out every day for messages, and the nearest shop was right beside where he stood. I see him still in my mind's eye—the gentle, sensitive face, the pale blue eyes seeming to look far into the distance. He was dressed in an ordinary fashion—old suit, cap, and shirt open at the neck. He was a thin man of medium height, and from a distance there seemed nothing unusual about him. But when you got nearer you would see a gentle smile on his lips, a quiet dignity about his person.

He never said much, this man from Clare, never tried to assert his personality, and yet there was a strength about him, an air of refinement which had nothing to do with background or education, but which was just his nature. Children from the area would gather round him, but, strangely enough, didn't jeer him as they did some of the inhabitants of the Iveagh. There was something about him which didn't lend itself to the casual cruelty of children. At another time, and in another place, he might have been lauded as a poet or a wise man but the Iveagh Hostel wasn't noted for the refinement of its clientele, and so he would inevitably be judged by the cut of his clothes and by his place of residence.

Sometimes when I passed by I would nod and say 'hello', and ask him how he was. His eyes would pull back from the distant horizons and gaze at me in a grave fashion, but still with a smile on his lips.,

'I'm well, and how is your poor mother?' He always said that—'your poor mother'. 'You'll do your best to look after her, won't you?' he asked. I knew for a fact that he had never met my mother—or my father either—so I was a bit puzzled by this. I nodded.

'Life is hard for poor people, and sometimes for rich people too,' he said, 'so don't hold it against your mother and father for being the way they are; remember, there's a reason behind everything.'

Cures

Sometimes a wife would be heart scalded with her husband's drinking. She might be talking to a dealer on Thomas Street about the freshness of her vegetables or rummaging through the bundles of clothes in the Iveagh Market when her frustration would boil over;

'I'm tellin' ya, Vera, that louser is goin' out and spendin' the money in the pub an' leavin' me short for the week.'

'Well, Sadie, that bowsie is like my brother, he's the same, sometimes. I think he's a bit wantin' like, not the full shillin'.'

'Well, I'm fed up to the eye teeth with my fella, an' I'm goin' to put a stop to his gallop tonight, so I will.'

People used to sprinkle holy water over an afflicted person in hopes of divine intervention. Novenas would be done and saints invoked to intercede on behalf of the sick person. In the case of a husband going out and spending money on drink, while he might go to Mushatt's chemist for a dose of the black draught to cure his hangover, his wife might be buying a bar of Brooklax laxative. She might save this for payday or dole day. There he would be, getting ready to go out to the pub to meet his cronies when his stomach would cramp and he'd have to make a dash downstairs to the toilet. There was no going out to the pub for him now, and besides, he would not be able to spend a good deal of the family money before his wife secured some of it for the week ahead. This was not done too much though—as the saying goes—you can take the pitcher to the well too often.

For some reason, constipation was a dreaded condition and everyone would have a supply of Brooklax or something similar in case anyone in the family should get 'bunged up'. Because of its chocolate-like appearance, mothers could fool small children into eating it. Having clean bowels was considered to be very important for good health.

There were all sorts of pills and powders which could be bought in the local shop, like Beecham's Powders and Beecham's pills. Mrs Cullen's Powders also claimed to be effective against all sorts of ailments including coughs and colds, influenza, neuralgia—the list went on, and it seemed that all they were short of claiming to cure was leprosy and the plague.

If all else failed there was always the paying of money to have a Mass said or the lighting of candles in the church in hopes of intercession by the saints or the Virgin Mary on the sick person's behalf.

Sheep's Head

There we were sitting around the kitchen table—the oil cloth covering it worn through in places where hot tea pots or cooking pots had been placed and been lifted off taking with them their share of oil cloth. My mother with the dresser behind her—no nice family heirloom this, no, a fifties dresser with its awful sliding patterned glass panels, its bottom doors complete with brass-painted knobs which sometimes closed properly and sometimes didn't, and the collection of mis-matched cups and saucers bought in a closing down sale or given away. They were displayed in the middle section as if they were a china collection. Then there were the three birds in flight over the fire-place, one of them hanging crookedly as if symbolically commenting on the state of our lives.

Anyway, there we sat—my mother, sister and myself waiting for my father to come home. This was dole day and my father had gotten away from the Labour Exchange on Werburgh Street with the money before my mother had a chance to nab him. All we had to eat all day was bread sprinkled with sugar washed down with tea laced with 'Springtime' condensed milk. You wouldn't need sugar in your tea with 'Springtime'—it was that sweet by itself. We waited and listened for the sound of my father's footsteps on the stairs. We always knew when it was him coming up the stairs to our flat, as because of his gammy leg his footfall made a distinctive sound on the concrete. It was now just past midnight and even though my sister and me were due to go to school the following day, we had stayed up late, partly to keep our mother company and partly because we were hungry.

In the past when my father had skived off with the money, he'd often shown up late at night with a parcel of fish and chips which he'd bought in Burdock's on Werburgh Street. Even though the fish and chips were stone cold, having been bought hours earlier and presumably been lying about on the pub floor, we would rip off the paper and devour the fish and chips. As my mother would remark; 'Hunger is a good sauce'.

In any case we were used to going hungry at least a couple of days a week as the dole money would run out after about three days and then it was back to the pawn — if there was anything left to pawn — or my father would mooch around trying to make a few shillings whatever way he could.

Sometimes he got a day's work at the cattle mart. This meant getting up very early — two or three o'clock in the morning and walking to the cattle mart on the North Circular Road. There he waited to see if a butcher needed a drover to herd the cattle or sheep he'd bought back to the abattoir for slaughter or to a plot of ground he might own near his own premises. My father would go among the animals marking them with red or blue or whatever colour raddle denoted ownership. The amount he was paid was only a couple of bob and sometimes a wrap-up of fatty meat from the butcher.

There was one time I remember when a neighbour informed on us to the Authorities. The situation was that if the Labour Exchange—Social Welfare—found out that a person got any other money, even if it was only a few shillings, then they were cut off the dole money for at least six weeks. The result of this 'neighbourly' action was that we were literally starving, living from hand to mouth for that period of time. I don't even want to think about these few weeks, and the desperate situation we found ourselves in. Suffice to say that we survived, and now here we were, waiting for my father to come home.

We sat there and waited, my mother getting more and more angry as hour followed hour. Finally my father's shuffling footsteps could be heard approaching the 'little' landing below.

'I wonder where oul Hopalong was till this hour,' my mother said. Of course she knew well where he'd been but she was just building up a head of steam for the coming confrontation. Anyway, in walked my father, his head down and something wrapped in newspaper under his arm.

'There ya are,' my mother observed, 'and what kept ya out till this hour of the night?'

'I got this for ya',' my father said, placing the peace offering on the table. He fished in his pockets and found a couple of sixpenny pieces and one half crown which he placed on the table beside the bundle.

'And what, may I ask, is that Joe boy? You're a quare lookin' boy all right.'

'Cathy, a fella in the pub said ya can make lovely soup out of that,' said he undoing the newspaper wrapping. And there it sat on the table, its hollow eyes seeming to stare at us in reproach. A sheep's head! There followed a silence which seemed to go on for ages but which in reality probably only lasted a minute or two. During this time not only could you have heard a pin drop but my mother's breathing could be heard getting more and more laboured and that was always a bad sign. My father of course being anaesthesised by alcohol wasn't able to read the signs very well and so his reactions were slower than they might otherwise have been.

'Make soup out of it, is that what you're sayin'? Make soup out of it,' she repeated, 'well, I'll give ya soup, ya hoor's melt ya, ya lavin's of a hoor!'

It seemed to be finally getting through to my father that all was not well on the home front. Belatedly he started to shuffle towards the door, vainly hoping my mother wouldn't see. It says much for his state of intoxication that he somehow thought she wouldn't notice. She stood there, arms folded across her chest, fixing him with a gimlet stare.

'Are ya goin' somewhere, Joe-boy?' she asked derisively. My father didn't know whether to say yea or nay, but no matter what he said at this stage it wouldn't have made any difference—his goose, or should I say his sheep's head, was cooked. Finally making up his mind that flight was the wisest course of action he made a bolt for the door. He almost made it through before a plate crashed against it, sending chips of delph over his cap and shoulders. If he could make it down the first flight of stairs and past the little landing, then he would be safe. My mother however, had other things in mind.

'Where do ya think you're goin'? Are ya goin' to look for the rest of the sheep be any chance?' Keeping his head down, my father kept moving towards safety. My mother meanwhile was looking for something more substantial to throw when her eye lit on the sheep's head reposing on the table. She ran after my father shouting all the while—'Ya forgot somethin', didn't ya? Here's your brother!'

And with that she flung the sheep's head—newspaper wrapping and all—at my father. The sheep's head caught my father on the side of his head and he went down in a crumpled heap on the little landing.

'There ya are now, 'head the ball',' my mother said. 'You go now and get your crony from the pub ta make soup out of that for ya.' The sheep's head meanwhile, following the impact with my father's head, had continued with its own momentum and now lay on its side gazing dully at my father who had managed to scramble half erect on the landing above. There was only a small trickle of blood on the side of his head and so it would seem that he and my mother would live to fight another day.

It would be another night spent in the Iveagh Hostel for him. The next day my mother would have cooled down and he would be able to negotiate a truce of sorts. We knew he would show up the following day, he always did, and for a while at least things would be peaceful.

Walks with my Father

One warm summer day in the fifties my father, my sister Mary and me were walking along by the canal. We were so excited to be away from the flat and also because we had our fishing nets on bamboo sticks and were sure we would catch some fish. We had our jam jars ready, too, and with the sun dappling the water everything seemed perfect. We also had our shopping bag full with everything we needed for the day.

Looking around we could see other people doing the same but we got ourselves a nice little spot on the bank of the canal and settled down to wait. It wasn't long before we had netted a few little fish we called pinkeens. These we put in our jars along with canal water. We held them up to the light and squealed with excitement to see them swimming around. My father kept having to shush us and he explained that there were fishermen further down the bank who took their fishing more seriously and that the noise we made could frighten the fish away.

After about three or four hours it was time for refreshment. We dug into our shopping bag and took out our sandwiches—thick crusty wedges of bread. Some of these were spread with dripping and some were sprinkled with sugar. My father had his milk bottle full with sweet tea and we washed our sandwiches down with a bottle of lemonade. Everything tasted delicious on that day and before we left we released our fish back into the canal. As the early evening came on, clouds of midges descended and we laughed as we walked through them, swatting them away.

On another occasion I went with my father as an apprentice cattle drover. We walked to the cattle mart on the North Circular Road and collected about a dozen cattle. This was my first time to be close with livestock and I was a little frightened at their size and their muscle movements as they plodded along. Of course, I didn't let my father know this—it seemed somehow wrong to show fear. My father had a stick and I had a smaller one to manage the cattle. Every so often one of them, sometime two, would decide to go in a different direction. Then it would be shouts of 'Hey-up!' and I would watch the general herd while he ran after the others.

We arrived at last at the abattoir. The first thing I noticed was the smell of blood and sawdust. My father chatted with the man who worked there and it was arranged that I would witness a cow being killed. I didn't want to see this but didn't know what to say as I knew my father meant this as a treat for me. The man approached the cow and produced a lumpy-looking metal thing. I had expected to see a Colt .45 like the cowboys used in the films. He held this against the side of the animal's head and squeezed the trigger. A bolt shot out and immediately the cow fell down, twitching on the ground, its eyes wild and frightened. I was so startled I jumped back, pale and shaking. It was decided I shouldn't watch what happened next.

Before we got home later that day, my father told me not to tell my mother what had happened. But of course my mother only had to take one look at me to see there was something wrong.

'What happened?' she asked me.

'Nothin',' I said.

She turned to my father.

'What did you do? Why is she so pale and shaking like a leaf?'

My father shrugged his shoulders and spread his hands out.

'I don't know, Cathy, maybe she's sick.'

My mother wasn't going to let this go; she kept on and on until she found out, when she ate the head off him.

'Well, ya dirty article, ye stupid reprobate!' she called him.

As for me, I felt doubly guilty. One, for getting my father into trouble and two, because of the cow. It took a while to get that image out of my head.

Sometimes my father and me started off to go to a particular place and ended up going to another. One day, we were supposed to go to collect newspapers to sell in town, but somehow ended up in a pub on Golden Lane. The barman, who knew my father well, frowned.

'Now Joe, you know we don't like children in the pub.'

'Ah Jerry, I'll just have the one and go.'

'All right so.'

My father smacked his lips as he looked at his pint of Guinness with its thick creamy head. I got a free glass of blackcurrant which was a great treat. Then on we went to a butcher's shop on Capel Street where my father plámásed the man into giving him a wrap-up of fatty meat. As we crossed the bridge I stood looking at the metal seahorses which decorated the bridge.

'Dad,' I said, 'where would you get to see them swimming?'

'Ah sure if you keep lookin' at the Liffey down there, you might see them leppin' up.'

Then he laughed and I knew he had been pulling my leg.

'You remember,' he said, 'the story your mother told you about your Uncle Mick?'

I pretended I didn't remember because I wanted to hear it again.

'Well,' he said, 'Mick was after comin' out of the pub and he was as drunk as a lord. He staggered over to the bridge here and leaned over the Liffey wall to get sick. As he was chuckin' up his guts, his dentures shot out of his mouth and went floatin' down the Liffey. Mick was left standin' there, with a stupid drunken look on his face. I'm telling ya that was a strange catch for some fisherman!'

We laughed and laughed until my stomach felt sore.

Then it was up towards City Hall and turning right to Christchurch Cathedral. We stopped for a bit and got chips wrapped in newspaper in Burdock's chipper on Werburgh Street. Then it was back to Christchurch and turn left down the cobbles of Nicholas Street hill until we came to Patrick's Park. There we sat on a bench and ate our chips and the little bag of crispy bits which Burdock's threw in for free.

We had to keep an eye out for the park keeper who had his lodge at the back gate of the park—there were loads of rules about what you couldn't do in the park. You shouldn't eat, spit, curse, play ball, cycle and many more. It was only a small park but on every bit of grass there was a metal sign saying—KEEP OFF THE GRASS. We did go over to the fountain and slake our thirst there.

Then we strolled around the corner of St Patrick's Cathedral to St Patrick's Close. Behind the railings were statues of past dignitaries of St Patrick's. As far as I can remember, most if not all of them were seated. Some had scrolls in their hands and all looked solemn and scholarly. There was one statue of a man who sat with his head leaning sideways on his hand.

'What's he doin'?' I asked my father. 'Ah, he either has a toothache, or he's waitin' for a shave.'

We giggled a bit and walked on past the stone horse trough into Kevin Street. Then it was a short journey home. On the way we bought a head of cabbage and spuds to go with the fatty bacon. My mother would be pleased enough with that.

The Boogie Man

'The 'Boogie Man' is comin' to get you if you don't go to sleep.' So threatened my mother to us children. Of course, the proper name for this frightening character was the 'Bogey Man', but in true Dublin fashion we twisted it into the 'Boogie Man'. We squealed and cowered under the coats which served as blankets, and every so often peeped out to see if the 'Boogie Man' really was coming.

'I saw him, I saw him, I swear!', my sister screamed, and we hugged each other in fear.

'What did he look like?' I asked her.

'Janey Mac, he's tall and skinny, an' his face was all white, an' he was floatin' over the floor, an' he had long black hair, an' he had his hands held out like he was goin' to grab us, an' his nails were all black.'

'Oh, Janey', I said, not questioning how she could have seen so much in one quick peek.

Matters weren't helped by the fact that we still had no electricity. We lay there, watching our one small candle burn down. The fire in the grate too, had burned low, and the pulsing light from the cinders cast moving shadows on the walls and ceiling. There were many places in the room where a Boogie Man or any other ghostly 'thing' could be lurking. The door was half open and it seemed now as if something was hiding behind it as it creaked in the draught which blew down the chimney. There was another full candle lying down beside the almost spent one and it was only three or four steps away to reach it and light it from the smaller one. But neither of us was willing to take those few steps and risk being grabbed by 'something'. It was then that we realised we badly needed to visit the toilet.

'Mammy,' we called out to the front room, 'Mammy, we have to go to the toila'.'

'What's wrong with yis at all, yis have me heart scalded, afraid in the dark like little babies, go on in there now, an' I'll wait in the door till yis come back.' Having tried to make us go asleep through fear, my mother was now reaping the rewards of her terror tactics.

I can remember many occasions when we sat around the fire, with the only light coming from the flames, listening to ghost stories. My father's favourite one was about the time when he was a young lad, and he and his friends were coming home late at night from a card school. They were all fearful already about what would happen to them when they got home so late. Added to this was the knowledge that they had been gambling and the apprehension they felt in case their parents—especially their fathers—had somehow found out about it. This was an offence punishable by a good few thumps.

In any case, there they were, slinking along the road, when their attention was caught by the sight of an old woman. She was sitting outside on a window ledge combing her long white hair with a strange, shiny-looking comb. The moon cast an eerie light on her and it was then they noticed the strange pallor of her face, and the fact that they couldn't see her eyes—so deep set were they in the sockets. A couple of the lads started to titter nervously. The old woman took offence at this and threw her comb at them. This was the signal for all-out panic, and they ran and scattered in every direction.

'It's the Banshee!' one of them shouted, 'don't let her hit ya with her comb or you're a gonner!' This warning was, my father recalled, too late for one of them, as the comb touched off his sleeve and fell to the ground. He screamed as if a red-hot poker had touched his skin. Whether it was coincidence or not this young man was dead within a year.

It was now my mother's turn to tell her story. She said she was sitting in the front room of our flat, when she heard three knocks at the door. She went immediately to the door and opened it but there was no one there. She was puzzled by this, as the landing outside was made of concrete and there had been no sound of footsteps. There were a few steps down from our landing to a smaller landing below and this could be seen from our door. There were no flats on this smaller landing so it was a mystery as to how anybody could disappear so quickly. She went back in and sat down.

To her surprise, the three knocks were repeated again. She went quickly to the door, thinking that maybe some children were playing games, and she was prepared to give them an earful. Once again there was nobody there and she began to be fearful. She quickly closed the door and had barely sat down when the three knocks came again. The hairs stood up on the back of her neck. She didn't want to open the door but something drew her over, and she found herself standing there with the door open. She said she'd never forget what she saw.

A small, young woman, dressed in nineteenth-century clothes stood there. She wore a shawl and bonnet and she seemed to be carrying something in her arms. She gazed steadily at my mother, as if trying to tell her something. It was when my mother's glance went downward, that she said her heart nearly stopped in her chest, for the young woman's feet weren't touching the ground, but floated a few inches above ground level.

As my mother watched, the little woman's image slowly began to fade until there was nothing to be seen. My mother went back inside and collapsed in a faint. When she recovered she went up to John's Lane Church and lit a few candles and said a few prayers for the woman' soul, for it was her belief that the poor woman's soul wasn't at rest because of some wrong done to her.

The next day my mother heard of the death of a neighbour. Ever after this, any time she heard the three knocks, even though she never saw the ghostly woman again, she expected to hear of a death. My mother always left out salt and water on the table on All Souls Night for the poor souls she believed had leave to be about on that night.

As time went by, we became a little more prosperous and didn't have to resort to candles quite so much. The light from a one hundred or one hundred and fifty watt bulb didn't lend itself to the telling of ghost stories and there were no dark corners any more in which a Boogie Man might hide. Still, sometimes late at night when a floorboard creaks or the wind comes moaning down the chimney, you could almost imagine a dark shape standing—waiting. Or when the moon hides behind a cloud, and the night becomes very still, there are strange sounds to be heard, if you listen very carefully.

Nancy and Dermo

I remember Nancy. There was a gang of us playing in the street. This was a time of large families and there was no room for the children to stay indoors during the day—the flats were places to eat and sleep in—so out on the street we swarmed and if it rained, well then, we would shelter in the hallways until the shower was over.

Some of us were swinging on a rope from a lamp-post. Some were playing 'picky' or hopscotch, while up the street a group were playing 'Relievio'. 'Relievio' was a game in which one child stood with her back to the others and threw a ball over her shoulder. She would then turn around and try to guess who was hiding the ball behind her back. The chant would go—'Relievio, who has the ball? Is she big or is she small? Is she black or is she white? Is she going home tonight?' If the first girl didn't guess right, then she would stay on 'it' until she did.

Up in the far corner—near Henshaw's yard—another group, mainly boys, were playing marbles. Their faces wore an intense look as they competed to win each other's marbles. Or even better still, the prized 'conker' or 'gullier'—the largest black marble.

One day, Nancy arrived. She was just suddenly there one day on the street.

'Who is she?' we whispered. Someone said, 'She's

the Slevins' cousin, out of the orphanage for a week's holiday.' There were fifteen Slevins, counting the mother, father and granny—in a one-bedroom flat.

We looked at her, nobody saying anything. In a world of poverty, she stood out as being worse off than we were. The first thing was her shaven head. But even more remarkable were the scabs that dotted her skull. Small, pale face, stick-like arms and legs which stuck out from a skinny body. Her dress was old-fashioned looking and buttoned up to the neck.

'Why has she got a scabby head?' someone asked. Biddy, Nancy's cousin, answered, 'That's because her head was infested with lice for a long time and it got infected and that's why they shaved her head.'

Nancy stood there, so still and quiet. It was as if she were afraid to draw attention to herself. I never remember hearing her speak, only saw her whisper to her cousins.

The most hurtful things I remember about Nancy were her eyes—faded blue, like an old person's—and the stillness about her. Later, seeing old news footage of concentration camps during the Second World War, I was struck by the resemblance in appearance between Nancy and some of the survivors of those death camps.

I remember Dermo too. A stocky little boy, seven or eight he would have been then, in the late fifties. Short trousers, always grinning. He was mischievous in an innocent sort of way. There was no malice in him. He came from a family of five brothers and sisters. His two older sisters mammied him a bit. His own mammy was ailing. I'm not sure what was wrong with her. She looked pale and gaunt, and in the way of children, I didn't think about it too much.

I remember him often having skinned knees. Always climbing he was, usually lamp-posts and walls. There were no trees in our part of Dublin city. Full of energy and youthful exuberance. His older sister often had to mend his trousers and stand up for him against the annoyance of his parents. The family were hard up for money, as were nearly all of us around the area, and couldn't afford to be buying new trousers. He had climbed all the other walls, lamp-posts and drainpipes around the area. Dermo was caught climbing the warehouse wall which was situated on the road where we lived. They put him into a reformatory 'school'. Six years he got for his 'crime', almost the length of time he was alive. Too far away for his family to visit, and in any case they couldn't have afforded the train fare.

From time to time a boy or girl would be missing from the crowd of children in the area. When we asked what happened to them we were told they had been 'sent away'. Often the reason for their being sent away to an industrial school was non-attendance at school or, in one case that I know of, the child had stolen apples from a priest's orchard. Or sometimes it was simply because they were poor.

Time passed and there were lots of events going on to take our attention. So apart from Dermo's family, I suppose the rest of us just carried on with our lives. Some years later I saw him walking down the street. Of course he was older and taller. It was a strange sensation to be looking at Dermo and yet not to be seeing him. His eyes were the same shape and colour as before, but there was something lacking there—the spark of joy, of youthful innocence was missing. There was a dullness, a . . . it's hard to describe. But it was like as if something had drained away his own self and left behind just a coating of what Dermo might have been.

Francis Street

Sam's Junk Shop was on Francis Street. That is what he called it, and that is what it was. No pretensions there. I remember as a child peering into the window and trying to see what was on offer. This wasn't easy as the window was dusty and the display was cobwebbed and overlapping. There were strange pieces of metal and wood whose use I couldn't fathom. The only things I recognised were the picture frames and strings of beads.

And then there was Sam himself, who was a member of the Jewish community. He sat just inside the door of his small shop. He looked like a huge bald-headed Buddha. The only thing was—his expression was far from Buddha-like. In fact, he managed to look world-weary and belligerent at the same time. If you wanted to go into the shop to try and untangle these tacked-up items, you would have to squeeze past Sam. I couldn't imagine doing that and then being trapped inside and having to squeeze past him again to get out. I never remember seeing Sam standing up.

Just down from Sam's shop was the Myra Bakery. Oh, the wonderful smells coming from the freshly baked bread and cakes! I can still remember the taste of the delicious apple tarts.

If we had a few bob, on occasion, we would saunter on a little and go into the Italian ice cream parlour. There we would sit in wonderful high-backed wooden booths and eat the delicious home-made ice cream drizzled with raspberry syrup and served in high glasses with long spoons.

On the opposite side of the street was the Tivoli Cinema. There, for a small fee you could get lost in the high drama of a Lana Turner or a Bette Davis film. Or sometimes the feature was a Western or horror movie. Conveniently situated beside the Tivoli was a sweet shop. There you could stock up on gob-stoppers or peggy's legs or sailor's chews. For long-lasting chewing though, you could buy a slab of Cleeve's Toffee. That would keep your jaw going right through the trailers, the B-movie and the main feature.

Up the street again and you came to the Church of St Nicholas of Myra—or Francis Street Church as the locals called it. It looked gloomy, or maybe my memory of it is tainted by what happened at my Granny Fitz's funeral.

Back up the street again and you came to the Iveagh Market. When you went in the front of the market there were many stalls selling old furniture. Further back and the middle section had second-hand clothes and shoes. The last part, which opened onto Lamb's Alley at the back, sold fish, meat and vegetables.

Adjacent to the Iveagh Market was a small pub. Back then, women were not allowed to drink in the bar. They were allocated space in the 'snug'. Snug describes it well as it was a tight fit for three or four women. There was a hatch in the snug through which the barman handed the women's drinks. There they'd sit in their black shawls and long aprons, sipping their glasses of porter. I remember once coming past the market and seeing two of the women coming out of the pub. They stood over the grating outside, their legs apart, hitched their long clothing up just a little past their ankles and letting the liquid flow down over the barrels in the cellar below. I remember thinking—ever practical—there must only be a man's toilet in the pub, and the women mustn't be wearing any knickers.

Then up the street a bit was Mushatt's chemist. The shop was tiny when you went in, but maybe it stretched a good bit back. Behind the high counter would stand one, or sometimes the two Lithuanian Jewish Mushatt brothers. The shop had wonderfully exotic smells and sights. There was an area at the back where the brothers made up their potions and lotions and medicines for every ailment. Up on high shelves behind the counter were beautiful large glass bottles filled with different coloured liquids. Some bottles were almost hour glass shape with big glass stoppers. When the light hit the bottles at a certain angle, they would glitter and sparkle with a wonderful glow. Then there were the labels on the bottles, long Latin names with here and there a hint of the exotic, bringing to mind faraway places like Arabia. The only label I recognized was 'Gentian Violet' which we bought for sores and scabs. The Mushatts themselves always kept up a high standard with their pristine white coats, their white, monk-like hair—even their faces glowed with a pink, fresh-washed look. Each wore half-moon glasses.

In those days, people went to the chemist for every ailment. The only time you would see a doctor was if you were in hospital. The Mushatts made up all their own medicines and ointments. They had treatments for everything from warts to ulcers, bronchitis to chilblains. They were famous for their brown plasters for a bad back and a different brown plaster for a bad chest. The Mushatts were very pleasant to deal with as they treated their customers with courtesy and respect. It didn't matter whether you were spending a penny or a pound, the treatment and smiles were the same.

At one time, I had warts on my hands and although they weren't painful, still, they looked terrible in my eyes and I wondered what to do about them. I also had scabs on my knees and my mother had lost patience with me over them. I had fallen some time before and cut my knees. I became fascinated with the resulting scabs and loved to pick at them and wait for them to form again. Of course this constant picking resulted in bleeding and the cuts never getting a chance to heal. When I complained to my mother about the warts she gave me a few pence and a couple of empty baby Power bottles and sent me up to Mushatt's. She instructed me to 'Ask for something to stop ye pickin' at them scabs while you're there.'

Anyway, when I got there I held up my hands for Mr Mushatt to see. He looked down at my hands with a solemn expression and made a tut-tutting noise and said; 'Ah yes, I have something to cure that.' He went into the back of the shop and emerged with a tiny bottle filled with a colourless liquid. The label on the bottle read; 'Wart Paint'. 'Dab that on a couple of times a day for a few days. Now, is there anything else I can do for you?'

'Well, me mammy told me to ask you if you could do somethin' about me scabby knees?' and I handed him up the baby Power bottles. 'Well, could you hold up your leg for me, please?'I did as instructed and he asked 'When did this happen?' 'About a week ago,' I lied. 'Hmm,' he said, taking the bottles, 'I'll make up some preparations to help with that; I'll be back in a few minutes.'

And he disappeared into the back of the shop again. When he came back he had two bottles, one had yellow liquid in it, and the other purple. The yellow one was labelled 'Iodine' and the purple 'Gentian Violet'. He told me to use the Iodine on my knees until the scab formed, and then to use the Gentian Violet. I thanked him and off I went home with the three bottles.

After a few days of using the wart paint, the warts fell off, never to return. After a few days of having yellow knees, followed by a few more with purple, I was cured not only of the scabs but also of the desire to pick at them.

School

John's Lane was my first school. I never knew the official name for it. It was down a lane-way beside Thomas Street church. Most of the girls attending the school came from Oliver Bond flats. The head teacher was a Miss McGrath. She was a striking looking woman — very thin, smartly dressed, usually in suits and with her brown hair loosely pulled back in a bun. Every morning she came into the classroom, walked up to her desk and took an egg from her bag. This she cracked into a mug, stirred it briskly then swallowed it down. This never failed to fascinate us as we had never seen anyone do the like of this before.

With Miss McGrath you felt that she expected you to do well. She wasn't one for showing emotions or physical displays but somehow you felt that she cared. Another thing about her was that she was always fair in her dealings with the children and this was very important. She was able to keep order without shouting and only very occasionally produced the cane. However, I never actually saw her use the cane.

One day I was picked from my senior infant's class and brought into a different room. This class was my sister's and was two years ahead of mine. I was to pick a name from a bag and whatever name I picked would win a prize. I misunderstood and stuck my head and all into the bag. Laughing, the teacher pulled my head back out, but I had managed to grab a piece of paper. Lo and behold, when the paper was unfolded, out of over thirty-five names I had managed to pick the one with my sister's name on it! This caused an uproar but it was judged that because the paper was folded, I couldn't have seen the name on it. Everyone was laughing and I felt so embarrassed. However, the teacher escorted me back to my room, patted me on the back and said — 'Good girl.' I didn't feel so bad then.

We learned how to write in Gaeilge and also a little Latin, including singing the Hail Mary in that language. We learned how to read and write and how to do sums. Arithmetic was taught from a table book. We chanted the tables in a sing-song fashion and it worked in the sense that it stuck in our consciousness. Weights and measures were taught in the same way. There were thirty-five to forty-five pupils in the classroom and those who couldn't keep up were put sitting down at the back of the classroom. At the end of ten years of school, some left without being able to write their own name.

The church we were brought to was very near—just up from the lane on Thomas Street. There were visits to the church to prepare us for our First Holy Communion. Also we were brought there for Benediction. There was a nice quiet atmosphere in the church and I loved the sound of the Latin being sung even though I didn't understand most of it. We had our little hymn books and it was peaceful to sing and hear the echo around the wonderfully decorated walls. The only trouble was I would sometimes faint after kneeling for a while. I don't know whether it was because of the smell of the candles and incense or maybe it was because I was anaemic.

After a couple of years I was in Miss Bolger's class. She was a red-haired lady with big teeth. She always had me sit up front of the class because I usually knew the answers and put my hand up. I was jeered by the other girls and called the teacher's pet. I learned not to put my hand up quite so much and keep my head down.

There was one occasion when the priest came to examine us in our Catechism. I was asked to recite the Ten Commandments. He asked me about the commandments which said: 'Thou shalt not covet thy neighbour's wife' and 'Thou shalt not covet thy neighbour's goods'. The question he asked me was: Which was the most important, the wife or the goods? After a few seconds of deep thought I answered 'The goods'. The priest roared with laughter, as did the teacher, taking her cue from him. I learned that sometimes you could be wrong, yet right at the same time.

Miss Bolger didn't have a cane; she had the leg of an old chair instead. This made quite a stout stick. She never used it on me but sometimes she would be standing near me and start shouting at someone behind me. Startled, I was afraid to look behind me to see who might be getting it with the stick. Strangely enough, my mother had the same habit of standing near me and suddenly letting a roar at someone else. There came a time after just such a situation with my mother when I started shaking. She became concerned and decided that it must be the teacher's fault. Up she marched to Miss Bolger's classroom and upbraided her about frightening me. Miss Bolger was apologetic and assured my mother she would make sure I understood that she wasn't angry with me.

I was mortified for two reasons, one was because it wasn't fully Mrs Bolger's fault that I was upset—there was constant shouting and rows at home—and two, Mrs Bolger, who had never shouted at me or touched me, began reassuring me every day that she wasn't angry with me. This did not go down well with the other girls in my class.

I have fond memories of John's Lane School and this is mainly because of Miss McGrath. She instilled a love of learning in me and also somehow managed to make the pupils feel that they were worthwhile—that their lives could amount to more than their current circumstances would indicate.

Shortly after we moved from the tenement room to a Dublin Corporation flat my sister Mary decided that she wanted to move school because she had friends in the other school. The teachers in John's Lane asked me to stay and pointed out that just because my sister was moving didn't mean I had to move too. But I was determined to follow my sister.

We moved to Whitefriar Street. Some of the girls attending were local and some were bussed in from Ballyfermot. We were poor but they were poorer. Once a week we were required to bring in at least a penny for the poor little black babies in Africa. The collection box sat on the teacher's desk and when you put in your penny the figure of a little black child perched on the box nodded its head in thanks. Sometimes the children, especially those from Ballyfermot, didn't have the penny. Then the teacher would upbraid and shame them in front of everyone. They hung their heads—those poor girls whose shoes were falling off them, whose large families didn't have enough to feed themselves—they were humiliated and made to feel even smaller than they felt already.

It was lucky that we got a sandwich and a small bottle of milk at school. On Friday, which was a meat-free day, we either got a currant bun or a cheese sandwich. On Tuesdays and Thursdays there were corned beef sandwiches. The corned beef was pressed really flat and along with being tasteless, sometimes had bits of gristle in it. Hungry as we were, sometimes we couldn't stomach it. Then some of the girls went round collecting the uneaten food to bring home. They said it was for the dog.

Cookery days were a bit of a trial for me. First of all we had to buy material to make our aprons and caps. Then we had to sew them up. Hours were spent using this stitch for this part and another stitch for that part.

Despite instruction from the cookery teacher I never did become a neat seamstress. She made soda bread to show us how baking should be done. It tasted awful and I thought—all that trouble to make something that nobody would want to eat. Then we were given a list of ingredients to bring in for cookery class. Some weeks I could get the money to buy these items and other times my family just didn't have the money to give me. On those days I began staying out of school so as not to be shamed in front of the class. After a while I began thinking it would be obvious why I was staying out so I began being absent on the day before too. This escalated to the day after as well until eventually I was summoned to court for non-attendance at school.

I realised on the day we went to court how powerless my parents were. Whatever was decided in that courtroom would come to pass and there was nothing they could do about it. Luckily, however, we got off with a warning. Some time later there was a second court appearance for the same reason. The teacher told the class in front of me that this time I would be sent to an industrial school. I was frightened because it was not unusual for this to happen. On this occasion the judge fined us one shilling. In school the next day the teacher asked me to stand up and tell the class about when I was to be sent to the industrial school. When I said we had been fined one shilling she became very angry and shouted at me to sit down.

At this time nearly every family who had girls named one of them Mary, so there was lots of Marys around. One Mary in particular I remember because of an incident in class. The teacher was absent from the class for a few minutes. There was a large clock on the wall at the back of the schoolroom and Mary decided it would be a funny thing to climb up on a desk and put the hands of the clock forward. She probably saw this done in a comic and in the story the outcome would be general hilarity with the teacher joining in. When our teacher came back she soon noticed the time had been changed on the clock. She shouted and demanded to know who had done this. All eyes went down and the tension built in the room.

There was a difference between a caning done for not knowing something and a caning when the teacher was really angry. At those times the teacher might ask you to hold out both hands and because she was angry the blows were more severe. At such times the girl would creep back to her desk holding her throbbing hands under her armpits in an effort to ease the pain. We never told our parents about being caned because we were afraid that we would be asked what we had done in order to be punished. We then risked getting a belt from our parents as well.

The teacher must have noticed something guilty looking about Mary because she pointed at her and shouted—'You, come up here' as she got out the cane.

Mary came up and stood before her. 'Hold out your hand' the teacher said as she swished the cane in the air. Mary stood there, her hands by her sides. 'Are you deaf as well as stupid?' the teacher screamed, a little spittle now appearing at the corners of her mouth. Still Mary stood there and I don't know if it was defiance or fear or a bit of both that made her resist the teacher.

'Right then, it's your own fault then,' and with this the teacher swung the cane and lashed Mary on the legs with it. Half a dozen times the cane rose and fell as Mary turned to run but then the teacher got her on the backs of the legs as well. As Mary crept back to her desk the red lumps were already starting to swell on her legs. Looking at her face I could see she was trying her best not to cry, but tears welled up in her eyes just the same. I looked away and stared unseeingly at the blackboard.

Mary was from a large family who lived locally. Her mother was a dealer—she sold fruit and vegetables from a stall on the street. Some people might have said she was a bit of a 'targer', that is she wasn't behind the stairs when it came to holding her own against anyone. Anyway, the day after the caning incident she came up to the school and called the teacher out. We could hear Mary's mother shouting and the sounds of a scuffle coming from the corridor outside. 'Mary's not able to walk today because of what you did to her!'

The teacher must have said something about the police because Mary's mother shouted—'Call the police then, I dare ya and while you're at it show them the big lumps on my daughter's legs! If you ever do anything like that again I'll streel ya down them stairs and I'll take that cane and bate ya back up with it!'

We sat in class grinning at each other but when the teacher came back in, her hair loose from her bun, her face red but not with anger this time, we looked down. After all, we didn't want to draw unwanted attention.

I don't remember much about Geography lessons apart from the teacher pointing out which were Catholic countries and which were not. Miss Slowey had an unusual view of weather patterns. She pointed to the map and asked us why was Ireland blessed with milder weather than England. None of us knew the answer. She then told us that despite Ireland being nearer to cold weather fronts than England, Ireland was especially blessed because we were Catholic. She said this with a hint of fanfare, beaming round triumphantly at us all.

Another memorable day was when we were in sixth class and Miss Slowey had us line up around the classroom. We looked at each other and wondered what was going on. Miss Slowey started talking about boys and girls and saying they were different from each other. I noticed that her face was getting red and it made her white hair stand out more. She talked about the proper way for girls to sit—that is with their knees pressed tightly together. We shouldn't cross our legs as this would give the boys a chance to glimpse our underwear.

We should dress and behave modestly at all times so as not to give the boys an occasion of sin. She now started mumbling and looking more and more embarrassed. The redness had now spread to her neck and this had the effect of making us feel very uncomfortable.

When I glanced around I could see the girls looking down at the floor. Some of them were trying not to giggle and were elbowing each other. The end result of this talk was general confusion. After Miss Slowey had fled the room we were unclear whether she meant it was better to wear slacks or a skirt in company with boys. She didn't explain which would be better at making it difficult for the boys to get at us. Anyway, what was clear from this talk was that boys were the enemy, to be treated with caution and suspicion. It was up to us girls to act and dress modestly at all times. Boys, it seems, couldn't help themselves. From the way Miss Slowey had acted and looked, I got the impression that she herself had lived up to these principles. Of course the word sex was never mentioned at all at all.

Butch the Whippet

It was around this time that I began pestering my mother to get a pup. We already had a cat, who was middle-aged. Of course I didn't consider what the cat might think of this. When talking in school about my hopes for a pup one of the girls from Ballyfermot piped up and said their bitch had just had a litter. She said I could have a pup for half a crown. I went home to my mother and launched my campaign. We got the money together and my mother told me on no account was I to bring home a bitch—they were too much trouble she said. A couple of days later the girl smuggled the pup into school. We hid him in a brown box in the toilets until school was over. So off I went home with my new pup. I can't remember whether it was the Dandy comic or the Beano where I got the name but the dog ended up being called Butch.

Every day I sallied forth with Butch, bringing him around the block and finishing up in Patrick's Park. First I looked to see if the park keeper was around and if he wasn't, I'd let Butch off the lead. He was a whippet and ran the circuit of the small park in extra fast time. After a few laps I put him back on his lead. The problem was that when I took him into one of the small shops he would wag his tail vigorously. Butch's tail was like a whip and people ran out of the shop squealing that their legs were being whipped. After that happened a few times it was decided that the tail should be docked. Opinions were given and the wisdom was that getting the tail docked would stop the dog from getting worms. So off with the tail and it was sad to see Butch still wagging his stump as he trotted along.

There came a time when every day I brought Butch for a walk we were followed by at least a couple of dogs, sometimes up to half a dozen. I kept having to shoo them away but they were very persistent. It was then discovered that Butch was a bitch! My mother went mad and threatened to have her put down. My pleading eventually averted the death sentence and a friend of my father's gave us some stuff to spray, saying it would put the dogs off. It worked up to a point and only an occasional very determined dog caused a problem. But we now had a dilemma—we had a bitch called Butch. It was too late to change the name now so from then on we were stuck with Butch the whippet bitch.

The Dispensary Doctor

The medical people came around the school. They were testing us for suitability for the BCG vaccination. They put a plaster on our chests and after a couple of days they came back to see if a rash had formed under the plaster.

This injection left a three-pronged scar on the arm. Because I didn't develop a rash, myself and my parents were sent down to the clinic on Lord Edward Street. Nobody spoke to me when I was brought into the room for treatment. No warning as to what was to happen. The nurse grabbed my arm and held it firmly. The doctor then inserted a needle into my wrist. He poked about a bit with my vein, still without saying a word. It was extremely painful and I left still not knowing what it was all about.

On another occasion the medical people went around the school taking samples of blood. Some weeks later we got a letter saying I was anaemic. The instruction on the letter was that I should bring it to my doctor. So around I went to the local dispensary doctor. The waiting room was full with people, mainly women. As each one came out from the doctor the women waiting asked 'What did he give ya?'

'Ah, them brown pills, same as the last time; sure, they look like horse tablets.' Another woman came out and was asked the same. 'The usual brown bottle a'medicine,' she replied.

'Well, ya know wha',' another woman said, 'he never gets up off his arse to examine anybody, I think he's afraid to touch us or somethin'. Maybe he dirtied his bib in some posh place and instead of sackin' him, they stuck him here with us.'

'Ya might be right there,' a little old woman said. 'He always has a sour puss on him an' looks like he doesn't want to be here at all.'

'Well, ya know somethin',' the first woman said, 'no matter what ya go in with, whether it be an ulcer or ya could have fuckin' leprosy, an he'd still give ya either the brown pills or the brown bottle.' All heads nodded in agreement.

When it was my turn to go in I was a bit nervous. There the doctor sat behind his desk looking at me over his brown-framed glasses. Silently I handed him the letter. He glanced down at it and looked up at me as I stood there waiting. He looked down at it again and looked at me. I waited and waited. He looked at the door. I took my cue and crept out and went home.

'What did the doctor give ya?' my mother asked.

'Nothin,' I replied.

'I'll go up to Mushatt's then an' get you a tonic,' and that was the end of that.

So at different times I was fed Neeve's Food and Parrish's Food to try to build me up. These supplements weren't deemed to be enough though and daily my mother came at me with a large spoon of cod liver oil.

Still, my bony frame resisted these attempts to fatten me up and I went through my childhood as skinny and pale as ever.

There were people in the area who were said to have secret recipes for potions and ointments. There was a woman in Newmarket who made a black oily liquid which was said to cure many ailments. It seemed, at the time, that every other option would be explored before going to the hospital. There was a superstition or belief from former times when many of the poor died from TB or even further back when mass graves were prepared in Glasnevin Cemetery for the cholera victims of the tenements, and a memory of a time when many of the poor died in childbirth in hospitals. Many people, especially the old were afraid to go into hospital and it was often said 'Once you go into that place, the only way out is in a box'. Even though in later years the situation had improved for the general health of the people of the area, still, people took comfort and had faith in the fact that their local chemists, people like the Mushatts and 'Daddy' Nagle were there to help.

Sometimes my mother would display her legs and point to the faint crater-like scars on them. 'Look at that,' she'd say, 'that's where I had ulcers and the doctors couldn't cure them, so I went up to Daddy Nagle's in Meath Street. He put his own ointment on plasters and covered me legs with it. He told me the plaster would get hard, but to leave it on for three days and to come back then for him to remove them. I declare to God when he took the plasters off, the ulcers came off with them, roots an' all. Daddy Nagle is a great man, so he is.'

There were three hospitals in my area of the Liberties. The Adelaide was only a ten-minute walk away, on Peter Street and the Meath Hospital was also in close proximity as was the Mercer Hospital. However, Dubliners seemed unable to pronounce the 'r' in Mercer's and one woman could be heard telling her neighbours 'I'm goin' to Messers to see about the Ulster in me stomach.'

One day my father fell off his bike as he came down the cobbles of Nicholas Street hill. He had to be helped home by the neighbours. He would never have made it up the three flights of stairs without help. He was in a lot of pain. He went to bed in the big double bed in the front room. My mother sent for the doctor and hoped he would come, because everyone knew he didn't like making house calls. Anyway, he did arrive and gave my father a sort of examination. That is, he leaned over and gingerly poked his leg a bit. He told my father the problem was a pulled muscle and that he should get up and exercise as much as possible. The poor oul' bugger tried to do as the doctor said and painfully hobbled down the stairs. When he collapsed on the street he was brought to hospital where it was discovered he had a fractured femur.

Most of the time we went to Mushatt's or Daddy

Nagle's for something to ease our aches and pains, rashes etc. Sometimes though we went to the Adelaide Hospital. When I reached puberty I didn't get pimples or acne but I did break out in boils all over my face. The biggest and sorest one was on the tip of my nose. I tried squeezing them out but they came back again. So off I went to the Adelaide. I was greeted by an exotic sight. An Indian doctor dressed in a sari and long white doctor's coat came out to see me. She squeezed out my boils which was painful but she was kind so that made it not so bad. Then she dabbed on antiseptic and gave me an injection. I don't know what was in the injection but the boils didn't return.

In those days—late Fifties, early Sixties, it was rare to see a foreign person. On my road a black man would occasionally walk through on his way to the College of Surgeons on Stephen's Green. A group of children would surround him and follow him down the road. A volley of questions would be shot at him—'Hey mister, where are you from, where are you goin'?' 'Why are you black?' Some of the children would try to touch his skin and feel his hair. Depending on the personality of the person, he would either look terrified and try to walk faster, or smile and answer as best he could.

Some time later I was looking at Pathé News in the cinema and saw some white people arriving at an African village. These villagers had never seen a white person before. The children of the village surrounded them and kept trying to touch their skin and hair. It reminded me of the way we had behaved back in the Fifties. Which just goes to show that people, especially children, are the same the world over.

Shopping and Pawning

Gordon & Thompson's on Thomas Street was a large store selling household items, and I remember that going there with my mother always seemed to be a big occasion, buying oilcloth or curtains. The shop assistant, usually a woman of mature years, took great care in measuring out the two and a half yards of oilcloth. This was heavy duty stuff as it had to be durable enough to last for a few years, covering our kitchen table.

My mother picked out which pattern she wanted and the assistant rolled out the approximate length from the huge rolls stacked up behind her. The measuring tape around her neck reminded me a little of a doctor's stethoscope. There was also a brass measure inset on her side of the counter, and with a flourish she produced the large scissors. I can still remember the smell of the oilcloth as she sheared effortlessly through it. Carefully, she folded it into a neat square then measured out the right quantity of brown paper. There was no hurry as she parcelled it up and with a different scissors, cut brown twine from a large ball; then tying it up, carefully criss-crossing the twine so there was enough slack that the parcel could be carried easily.

Next came the grand finale when it was time to pay. My mother counted out the money into the woman's hand and watched as she pulled a lever and a 'cup' came whizzing down from the criss-cross of pulleys above.

She unscrewed the top of the cup, placed the money and the sales docket inside, screwed the top back on and pulled the lever again. This sent the cup flying up in the air on the pulleys, to a small box-like office with glass sections. The office seemed stuck on its own, high up on the wall. The woman seated there removed the docket and money, replaced them with change and a receipt and pulled her lever to send the cup gliding back down to the assistant waiting below.

With a feeling of satisfaction, we sallied forth onto Thomas Street. Right across the road was John's Lane Church. Sometimes we would go in and light candles for the poor souls in purgatory. The church had a nice feeling in it—calm and still. The only thing was the smell of candles and incense made me feel dizzy and for this reason I was relieved when we would emerge into the sunlight. Then, if there was enough money left, we would go around the corner onto Francis Street and my mother would buy a delicious ice cream cone from the Italian ice cream parlour. I can still taste that delicious creamy coolness drizzled with raspberry syrup.

Another memory is of a different sort of 'shop'—the pawn shop on Winetavern Street. Of course, everyone knew what it was, with its three large brass balls hanging up outside; everyone around went there but no-one wanted anyone else to know. Monday morning was the busiest time in the pawn as any money available would have been spent over the weekend. Then it was time to get out the man's suit and inspect it for any stains or marks which would decrease its pawn value. Much rubbing and scrubbing would take place to hide these potential loss-makers. The suit would be 'redeemed' on a Friday for the weekend and the woman would hope there would be no disastrous spillage to ruin its pawnability on Monday. Everything was brought to the pawn—clothes, bedding, and for the women the lowest point was if they had to pawn their wedding ring.

For me the pawn shop held a mixture of shame and fascination. We waited until the Monday rush was over in the hope that we could avoid seeing anyone we knew there. My mother often pawned the blankets given to us by the St Vincent de Paul, still in their see-through wrapping and easily identifiable, being grey with big red stitching on the borders. They were made of rough wool and because we didn't have sheets, sleeping with them next to your skin kept you awake itching at night. Then it would be coats on the bed as usual. Sometimes in the winter, the coats would be so heavy that it was hard to crawl out from under them. Anyway, we had to pawn the blankets as it was a toss-up between eating or keeping warm.

When we went inside, I was fascinated by the atmosphere—the huge vaulted ceilings, the long mahogany counters and the buzz of activity. There was a wooden spiral staircase and the employee went running up and down to disappear behind the covered wooden partition. High above were the same pulleys and wires as in Gordon & Thompson's, only in the pawn shop they were much more elaborate. Wires and pulleys went in all directions, and there were two or three people seated high above, dealing with the dockets and money.

There were favoured ones among the employees—those who dealt more leniently with the customers. Knowing this, queues formed in front of Jimmy and Stan; the other men drew those who were sure of the quality and cleanliness of their offerings. Jimmy would open the parcel at one end and fold back the clothing, but he didn't look too closely for cigarette holes or stains.

His opening offer 'Ten bob' received the expected reply of 'Ah, go on, Jimmy, ye gave me a pound the last time.' 'Ya must a been dreamin' or somethin'. I'll tell ya what; I'll stretch to fifteen shillings.' 'Ah, go on then,' and the deal was done to everyone's satisfaction.

Then he would fill out the docket, staple a duplicate of it on to the parcel and hand over the money. Sometimes though, the queue for Jimmy and Stan cleared quickly and the women were beckoned over to the other two men. I remember the look on the women's faces—as if they were criminals going forward to be sentenced. Sometimes my mother was among them. The examination of the parcels was much more thorough here.

'Ah, here missus, ya can't expect to be paid money for that,' as he displayed the stained cloth or stuck his finger through the cigarette burn. With a sneer, he'd push the parcel aside and call out 'Next!' The humiliated women crept out, heads bowed, clutching their parcels. The remarks they made reflected their disappointment. 'That fella wouldn't give ya the skin off a grape.' 'Yeah, I know, he wouldn't give ya the steam off his piss.'

And off they went down the street. Some other means of getting money would have to be found.

On the Never-Never

We had got a new bed for the front room—a double bed. It was great to get new things like beds and tables etc. but of course they had to be paid for. We always started off with good intentions but circumstances intervened in our ability to pay for them. The dole money usually ran out midweek and then my father would hustle about trying different ways to get money. Sometimes it would be selling newspapers, other times car park attendant, or occasionally a cattle drover. But these jobs were not reliable and so it was not possible to plan a weekly budget. Some weeks there was nothing available for my father. Then we would fall behind in the payments to the furniture company. In those days the companies mustn't have been talking to each other because we got furniture from the Star Furniture Company on Camden Street and then couldn't pay them. Then later, we got stuff from Cavendish's on Grafton Street with the same result.

Then there were the local shops. We and others around the area got groceries 'on tick' or 'on the slate' which were to be paid for on Friday of a working week or in our case on dole day. This arrangement was set up by the mothers but ever after that the children would be sent for the messages and the shopkeeper would write it down in the ledger. This worked out well for some weeks until something, often a small extra expense, showed up. Then everything went out of kilter. So we would have to 'do' the shopkeeper and hurry past to go up the road to the next shop. Then the same thing would start off again. Once something went wrong with the money, it never seemed to happen that we could get back on our feet again. After some time had passed we went back to the first shop and were able to get credit there again. It says much for these small shopkeepers that they allowed this, and they must have written off quite an amount over the years in our area alone.

Then there was the cheque woman. She called around every week and I can't remember whether the credit company she worked for was called Jordan's or whether this was a shop in the scheme. The big drawback of these cheques was that they could only be used in one or two shops. These shops were much more expensive than if you had the freedom to go to, say, Frawleys or Guiney's or Clery's. Another thing, from a young person's standpoint, was that we considered the clothes in the 'cheque shops' were 'Mary Hick' or 'Hickey' — meaning that they were old-fashioned. I do remember going with my mother to the cheque shop on Parliament Street and not liking anything they had. But beggars can't be choosers as the saying goes and the clothes would be 'falling off us' long before the cheques, with interest, were paid for.

The 'cheque woman' was very prim and proper and was always well dressed in suits and with her hair coiffured in place like a helmet. The look was finished off with a silk scarf tastefully draped around her neck and shoulders. Each week there would be a different scarf to blend in with her outfit. She would stand just inside the door and express her opinion on politics and religion and anything else that occupied her thoughts. Of course we had the usual pictures of the Pope and Jesus hanging on the wall. The Child of Prague too looked down on us from the ledge above the door. The holy water font was hanging from a nail just inside the door.

What the 'cheque woman' didn't know though, was that my family regarded these holy relics as weapons to ward off evil. If my mother heard an unusual sound, especially at night, she would sprinkle the holy water around to keep the evil spirits away.

The cheque woman admired our picture of the pale-skinned, blond, blue-eyed Jesus. She went further and declared that you would know a Protestant to look at as they always had brown eyes. Real Catholics, she maintained, always had blue or green eyes. As she was saying this I noticed that she had brown eyes. Also, all my family had brown eyes. This puzzled me and I kept looking at her to try to understand what she meant. Did this mean we weren't real Catholics, only pretend ones? And what about her—a staunch Catholic? This and other things were, for me, difficult to fathom. At Mass we were told that 'the meek shall inherit the earth' and 'blessed are the poor'. Looking around me it was hard to see in what way we were blessed. It seemed we would have to wait until after we died to reap the rewards of our poverty.

Messages

It was Easter time in 1958 and we children were playing on our road, which was off Patrick Street. The only traffic was a very occasional car, which passed down the road. Apart from that, we were more accustomed to seeing horses and carts. Of course, there were more cars than that in Dublin, but living as we did on a small road it was still relatively traffic free. There was only one family in the whole of our area that owned a car. You can well understand then, that when there was a draw for a car run by John's Lane Church, and that the winner of the draw turned out to be that very same car owner, it was the cause of much comment.

'Oh, have it and you'll get it,' some were heard to remark. 'There's more to that than meets the eye,' Mrs Byrne said. 'I know me own know,' said little Mr Brady, tapping the side of his nose.

We children listened to all of this but we didn't understand why anyone on our road should want a car — it was as far removed from our daily lives as a space rocket might be to a child today. And in any case, wasn't it much more fun to tie your rope to a lamp-post and swing away, or to play 'pickies' or hopscotch? We were more excited than usual because it was only a couple of days away from Easter Sunday. All our talk centred around Easter eggs and how many we might get.

There were many large families in our area. In some

cases there were twelve or more children and their parents living in a one-bedroomed flat. The Slevin family and one of the Byrne families even had a granny living with them as well. Anyway, there we were—a gang of us playing Relievio when Granny Slevin stuck her head out of the window of her second floor flat. We scattered as fast as we could to avoid being called to go for a message for the old woman. The usual thing was that we would be in competition with each other to run errands because it meant being rewarded with at least a penny and sometimes more. None of us, however, wanted to disturb our game to go for a message for Granny Slevin. The reason for this was that she seemed to have little idea of the going rate for anything. She seemed to be stuck in a time of her own choosing. On this occasion I was the unfortunate one left standing there when all the rest had bolted for their hall doors.

There was nothing else for it but to go up the stairs to see what she wanted. She stood on the landing—this little woman with her grey hair pulled back in a bun, her narrow frame covered in a navy blue crossover apron which had tiny flowers all over it.

'Will ya get me some snuff like a good child?' she said as she handed me sixpence. I went down to the tobacco shop on Patrick Street and asked for sixpence worth of snuff. When I was climbing the stairs back up to the granny's flat I wasn't expecting much in the way of a reward. This was because on a previous occasion she had rummaged in her apron pocket and produced a farthing. Even back then a quarter of a penny wouldn't get you much, if anything. She had a surprise in store for me this time, though.

She rummaged again in her seemingly bottomless pocket and produced a small statue. The statue looked old and smelled of snuff. I had to look closely at it to see that it was a likeness of the Virgin Mary. I don't know what expression I must have had on my face but whatever it was the granny looked at me and exposed her gums in a wide grin. 'That'll bring you luck, daughter,' she said. I stumbled back down the stairs and onto the street, clutching the little statue in my hand. The other children, who now felt safe to be on the road again, surrounded me.

'What'd she give ya, go on show us!' they chanted. When they saw the statue they howled with laughter.

It was different when you went for a message for your own mother. You didn't expect to get money then. My mother would often send me over to my father where he car-parked on Digges Street. Sometimes I would have to go back twice as he wouldn't have taken in enough the first time to pay for that day's dinner. The amount was always the same—five shillings. First, I would go to the vegetable shop on Patrick Street and get a quarter stone of potatoes and an onion. Then it was up the street to the corner shop to buy a half-pound of sausages, a few streaky rashers and a packet of oxtail soup. I hurried home to my mother with the makings of a coddle. Of course, if we'd had more money our coddle would have had more ingredients such as white pudding maybe, to thicken the soup, or some people would have put kidneys in the mix.

I remember the day I went as usual to the corner shop for the same ingredients. There was a new owner in place behind the counter of the tiny shop. There he stood, resplendent in his immaculate white coat—a young red-haired countryman. Previous owners of the shop had given items on tick if they knew you well enough. The new owner, though, was not interested in this way of doing things. His was strictly a cash-only business. This time, when I asked for the usual things, he told me the items came to five shillings and a halfpenny.

We looked at each other and finally he said, 'Make sure you bring it along the next time.' To me it seemed like a huge dilemma to find that extra halfpenny. This man, we heard some years later, went off and bought a mini-market. Of course, this news could not pass without comment. The general consensus was 'that fella still has his Communion money'.

The Seagull

I remember often awakening to the sound of the sea-gulls' cries as they fought over scraps of bread. They frequently perched on the high wall which faced our back window. Between that and the sound of the bells of nearby Christchurch and St Patrick's Cathedral we had a right mixture of sounds. On this particular day my mother's raised voice was added to the racket.

'Get up Joe, get up quick!'

'What's wrong?' my father asked.

'Will ya hurry up outa dat and get your trousers on, you've to go to the police station.' My father hurried out of the bedroom, looking alarmed. My mother was in the front room looking out of the window by this time. She turned around and beckoned my father over.

'There's a poor seagull with a broken wing on the road and ya'd better get down to the police station and get them to bring it for treatment.'

'Are ya mad or wha', Cathy?' he said, 'I didn't even have a cup of tea yet.'

'Never mind the tea, if ya don't get down there quick them childer'll torment the poor thing.' My father did as he was bidden and hurried down to the police station on Kevin Street, which was less than a ten-minute walk away. The street, meanwhile, had taken on somewhat the appearance of a scene from the Wild West with children cheering and adults acting like matadors trying to grab the seagull with coats and blankets. The next excitement was the arrival of a squad car with two policemen in it.

The two men stepped out of the car and we saw that one was older and experienced looking and the other looked to be only a lad. The older one folded his arms across his chest and addressed the crowd. 'Now who might be the owner of this seagull?' he asked. There was sniggering among the crowd. My mother stepped forward and told them that it was their duty to bring the bird for treatment. The older policeman decided that it was the younger man's work to catch the seagull which, broken wing or no, was determined not to be caught.

The younger man removed his jacket and eyed the bird, presumably to decide on his tactics. He obviously decided that surprise was the best policy. With a sudden flourish he threw his jacket over the seagull. The startled bird made a run for it trailing the policeman's jacket up the road. We then saw the bird, jacket and all, turning the corner onto Nicholas Street.

By this time the whole street was in a state of pandemonium and we followed the hunt around the corner. The older policeman seemed to be getting as much fun out of this as we were. The, by then red-faced, younger policeman made a flying tackle of a jump and succeeded in grabbing the seagull which was still wearing his jacket. A cheer went up from the crowd and the poor man must have felt he was in Lansdowne Road.

The bird, however, not realising his good intentions, twisted its neck around and began attacking his arm with its beak. He yelped and jumped but somehow managed to keep a grip on the bird. It was only then that his companion decided to lend a hand and between the two of them they managed to place the seagull in the boot of the car.

We were delighted with the novelty of all this. We hadn't seen this much excitement since Mrs Carey had fallen from her second floor window. Mrs Carey had stood up and walked away unscathed but the poor unfortunate man who happened to be passing by at the moment when she landed suffered a broken collarbone.

Anyway, my mother admonished the two men to treat the seagull with gentleness and to make sure that it got treatment for its injuries. She made no comment, however, when her eye fell on the younger man's beak-reddened arm. Off they drove, and the older policeman waved to us as they went, still grinning away.

Easter Eggs and Games

The bells of nearby Christ Church rang out and it seemed to me to be a lonely sound. Even when St Patrick's Cathedral bells joined in there was still an echo of something sad about it. This was Easter-time in 1958 and I suppose it was a time of joy in a spiritual sense, but we were not really thinking too much about spiritual things. It is true we had been hearing in school all about Jesus, and how he'd been in the tomb for three days and three nights and then had risen from the dead, but we weren't really paying too much attention to all that.

No, what was firmly fixed in our minds was that Easter Sunday was only a couple of days away, and that meant Easter eggs! On previous Easters our bounty of eggs depended on what was happening on the home front—whether my father was able to 'mooch' a few shillings here or there, or whether the lure of the pub had resulted in him arriving home in mellow mood, but with empty pockets. We children learned early on to be philosophical about it. That is to say, we learned not to show our feelings and disappointments too much. We knew that if we made a big thing about either getting no eggs or a very small one, our mother would feel bad and this would be translated into even more anger against our father and we wanted peace in the home at any cost.

When we played with the other children from the road, the talk was all about Easter eggs and how many each child hoped to get. Our play area was the 'alleyio'—a yard at the back of the flats. One part of the yard was given over to washing lines and the rent office. But there was a slopey part up at the back which had high walls on either side and a railed part which looked out on Werburgh Street. It was here, near the left-hand side wall that we had set up 'shop'.

The 'shopkeeper' was a girl called Patty and she ruled her premises with a stern eye for barter and protocol. For money we used 'chainey'—bits of broken delph which were highly prized. Brown or dull-coloured chainey was of lesser value than more brightly coloured bits, and these also were used in place of money. The most highly prized of all was bits of blue and white china—as can be imagined these were hard to come by in the Liberties.

In any case, there was Patty ruling over her shop which was perched atop an old wooden box, covered over with newspaper. On a part of the wall behind her she had set out her wares, using natural hollows in the wall to display the goods. Shiny paper and brown paper were used to wrap various sized stones which were imagined to be different types of food. There was great excitement when an empty lipstick case or powder compact was found, as one of these could be traded for any number of other items. Another much desired object was an empty shoe-polish tin as this could later be used to play 'picky'—a game of hop-scotch where numbered boxes were chalked on the ground and the child hopping on one leg would endeavour to kick the 'picky' from one box to another. If she kicked it outside the lines then she was 'out' and it was the next girl's turn.

When an empty Lavender Furniture Polish tin became available there was great excitement as this was much bigger than the usual 'picky'. Not only that, but the child who came out of her flat with such an item did so proudly as this showed her mother polished the furniture, and furthermore that there was sufficient furniture in the flat to warrant the purchase of such a big tin of Lavender.

'What'll ya give me for these?' asked Betty, a red-haired girl, holding out three marbles of various sizes and colours. There was a large steel-coloured marble called a 'steely', a big coloured one called a 'gullier' and a normal sized one. Betty was from a large family of fourteen, nine girls and five boys. All but three of them were red-haired. Patty looked at the marbles and appeared lost in thought for a while. Finally she made up her mind. 'I'll give ya a half pound of butter and four ounces of tea.'

'Wha'?' said Betty, 'I'da tha' you'd at least give me milk for the baba.' Betty held out her raggedy doll with its missing arm.

'Well, all righ' then,' said Patty, 'an' I'll throw in a coupla sweeties as well, how's tha'?' 'All righ' then.' Just as the business was being concluded a small red-faced boy came rushing up. It was Betty's brother Christy.

'Wha' are ya doin' with me marbles? Ya robbed them on me so ya did, give them back!' Betty tried to hold onto the marbles by closing her fist tightly around them but her brother prised her fingers loose and got the marbles. 'Oh ya hurt me ya did, ya little get ya!' Betty whined. 'Well, ya shouldn'ta taken them should ya!' Christy went running off before Betty had a chance to recover.

Betty spent a while twisting her cardigan around her hands and sticking her fingers through the holes. 'How many Easter eggs are ya gettin'?' she asked Patty. 'I don't know, me ma won't tell me.' 'I'm gettin' three,' Betty announced. Patty looked at her.

'How are ya gettin' three Easter eggs an your da's not workin?' 'Me uncle Jemser is comin' over with one anyway,' Betty bragged. 'I never knew you had an uncle Jemser, is he your ma's brother or your da's?' 'He's me ma's—no, I think he's me da's.'

'Do ya mean to say ya don't know?' Patty asked in mock surprise—her hands on her hips, trying to imitate her mother. 'Go on, ya liar ya, I'll see ya on Easter Sunday, an' ya can show me your three eggs.'

'All righ' then,' said Betty as she crept away.

Needless to say, the shiny coloured wrapping paper on Easter eggs was saved and used later in our games of shop when stones would be wrapped up in it as pretend sweets. Another use stones were put to was in a game called jack-stones. Stones of a certain shape and size were used in this game. First, the boy or girl would hold four stones clenched in the hand while the fifth was flipped in the air. The child would then endeavour to catch the stone on the back of the hand while still holding the other four. The game progressed until all five stones had been caught on the back of the hand. The next and final stage of this game was called 'fingies'. If a child was lucky enough and skilled enough to reach this last lap, the tension would be high as he or she placed a stone between each finger and tried to throw the fifth stone in the air and catch it on the back of the hand without letting any of the other stones drop.

This, and many other games, absorbed our attention and helped keep us occupied while we were growing up. We walked a lot, too. Sometimes it would be to somewhere near like Thomas Street, or more rarely into town.

The Bayno and other places

The Bayno Play Centre was only a couple of streets away on Bull Alley. Its proper name was 'The Beano' — meaning feast but it became known locally as The Bayno. It was one of the many facilities provided by the Guinness family through the Iveagh Trust. There was an outdoor playing area with a monkey puzzle, climbing frame, a roundabout and swings. The noise of children screaming with excitement was deafening. I remember climbing too high on the monkey puzzle and getting stuck — I could neither go up nor down. Standing there shaking and clutching the bars, I thought I would never get back down on the ground. Eventually I got down, carefully and slowly. There were many large rooms in the Bayno where various activities took place such as art, needlework, dancing and singing and for the younger children there were colouring books. On Saturday mornings there was sports and the girls were given a ball or skipping rope. The boys were given a football and an area to play in separate from the girls as at that time girls were not allowed to play football.

On some days in the Bayno we girls sat around a large table in a big high-ceilinged room cutting out figures from ladies' magazines. Looking at the ladies in the magazines was like seeing a whole different way of life. There they would be — always smiling as they lifted a freshly baked cake from the oven, or sat around with other ladies knitting or sewing. Sometimes the ladies would be waiting at the door to greet their husbands as, briefcase in hand, he arrived home from work. On every occasion they would be perfectly groomed with not a hair out of place. Even when they donned an apron in the kitchen it would be a fancy frilled affair. The children too, in the magazines—nearly always a boy and a girl, looked happy and clean. They would be depicted standing by the kitchen table looking with wonder-filled eyes at the perfectly baked cake as their mother stood by with a glow of satisfaction. This was all far removed from our lives but as we sat there slowly and carefully cutting out the figures there was a sense of peace and the lady overseeing us gave off a firm but kindly aura.

Part of the Bayno experience was the receiving of our shell cocoa in white enamel mugs with blue rims and accompanied by a bun. The buns were supplied by Kennedy's Bakery on Patrick Street. The big hall would be filled with children enjoying their buns and cocoa and occasionally a child would try to steal a bun from another and there would be a scuffle but one of the ladies would intervene and sort it out. There was never any corporal punishment—the only discipline was a disapproving look and this was enough to keep order.

Then there was the much anticipated Christmas party. The main hall would be decorated and each child received a gift. This was much appreciated as some children were unsure whether Santa would be able to visit their home that year. We were so excited and were very careful when opening the presents so as not to tear the lovely wrapping paper. This would be saved to be taken out and looked at later. On leaving the party we were given a big bag of sweets each. These were no ordinary sweets in the sense that the likes of them were never for sale in our local shops, and oh, the fanciness of them and the delicious taste! Proudly we took them home to display and to share.

The thing I remember most about the Bayno was the ladies themselves. They always seemed to be even-tempered and dressed often in twin sets and pearls, tweed skirts and nice leather shoes, smelling of talcum powder and face powder; they seemed to me like a different species, like aliens from another planet. But if so, they were, or so I felt, kind and wise aliens.

St Stephen's Green Park was a short walk away and we went there every now and then to explore the many nooks and crannies and to see the ducks. It was so much bigger than our more local Patrick's Park and had such a variety of plants and flowers. Sometimes the boys from our area followed us in order to look out for us. They would keep their distance but also keep us in sight. There were dangers too as some of the ponds had a lot of plants and grasses covering the surface of the water and from a distance you wouldn't know there was water beneath. There was one occasion I remember when we were walking along and we didn't notice that Bernie was missing. When we looked back we saw Bernie walking into the pond and to our horror saw her sink beneath the water. We ran back, but the boys, who had hung back, got there first and waded in and pulled her out. Bernie was shaken and dripping wet but otherwise she was fine.

Dublin Castle was a place we liked to explore. Walking down the cobbles of Little Ship Street, passing the three or four cottages on the left and the public toilets just beyond them, we arrived at the back gate of the Castle. There were many interesting twists and turns in the grounds but one of our favourite places was a high smooth wall where we played handball for hours on end. Sometimes when we walked through Dublin Castle we would encounter priests passing through in the opposite direction. These men often smiled at us in a fatherly fashion and one in particular was memorable for the fact that he looked just like a picture of a saint— white border of hair around his otherwise bald head, long brown robe, and a white rope-like belt. This priest or monk always stopped and smiled and whispered a prayer or blessing. Then he patted us on the head and passed on. After he left we looked at each other and giggled but felt affected by his presence all the same. We didn't know the history of Dublin Castle; to us it was just another place to play.

St Audoens Church on High Street was another place of interest to us. It seemed somehow different from the other churches and although it wasn't as big as some, it seemed to have a mysterious air about it, standing alone and back from the road as it did. It also had a large stone holy water font. Beside the church was a small railed grassed area and it was pleasant on a warm day to sit picking daisies and making daisy chains. Beside this was the forty steps. These wide stone steps looked very old and it took two steps to walk down each one. About two thirds of the way down this shaded area was a type of grating in the ground and someone had told us that this was where dead bodies were kept. We dared each other to bend down and look through the gaps in the metal cover. There was much screaming and squealing as one or two brave souls crept near and shouted 'I seen it, I seen it, there's coffins down there!' Even though most of us hadn't looked, we all became afraid and ran down the rest of the steps out onto the sunlight of Bridgefoot Street. It was on Bridgefoot Street that we sometimes encountered 'Bang Bang'. We felt cheated if he ignored us and would shout at him—'Go on Bang Bang, why don't ya shoot us?' He would oblige and take out his large key which he used as a gun and 'shot' us, all the while shouting 'bang bang!' Some of the children hid behind walls and pretended to shoot back and there was great fun and laughter to be had and 'Bang Bang' laughed along with us.

Mr Carbury Dies

There was one Easter that I particularly remember because it was the one when Mr Carbury died. Mr and Mrs Carbury were an old couple who lived opposite to us on the same landing. We, as children, hadn't been aware that Mr Carbury was sick. The only indication that something out of the ordinary was happening was the number of neighbours calling to their door and the way they talked in hushed whispers. My mother said that Mr Carbury was in heaven and that we should pray for his soul. I wondered why we needed to pray for his soul if he was already in heaven but I didn't say anything. Mrs Hughes—the widow woman who lived underneath, spoke to my mother—'I laid him out last night and he looks lovely, all peaceful like.' My mother gave the expected reply.

'You did a great job, Mrs Hughes, ya have great hands, may God reward ya for your goodness.'

Mrs Carbury came to the door and looked at me. 'Won't ya come in and see him, alanna?' I was terrified. I had never seen anybody dead before but I just knew I wouldn't like it. She led me into the back room where Mr Carbury was laid out. I had never paid much attention to him when he was alive but now I couldn't tear my eyes away from his still form. He looked much longer then I remembered and the colour! Such a waxy colour he looked with the rosary beads twined around his long fingers. As I stared at his face I was holding my breath in case he should move, in case his eye-lid should twitch. But nothing of the sort happened and I was aware of Mrs Carbury standing just behind me — waiting for me to say something. I racked my brain to think of something to say for I knew it was expected of me and at last I thought of something.

'He looks the image of Saint Albert, Mrs Carbury.'

'Do you think so?' she asked.

'Yeah,' I lied. 'I was lookin' at a book of pictures of the saints an' Mr Carbury is the spittin' image of Saint Albert.' Mrs Carbury seemed delighted and told my mother who looked at me and nodded.

'Aye, she's always lookin' in buks all right.' Mrs Carbury pressed a half-crown into my hand saying — 'You'll say a prayer for him, won't you?' 'A'course I will, Mrs Carbury.'

A half-crown! Two whole shillings and sixpence! I felt like jumping in the air but had to restrain myself with Mrs Carbury standing there. Of course I knew I wouldn't be able to keep it. We were short of money and I knew my mother needed it so I didn't even think of keeping it for myself. Besides, the next day was Easter Sunday and the shops were still open, so there was time for my mother to get some Easter eggs for myself and my sister, or to get more if we had some already.

Santa Claus

Over the years we had acquired many items on the 'never never' and my mother was often busy dodging the 'bill men'. We didn't actually own our furniture, or we never felt we did, as every other week another letter would come, threatening court proceedings or seizure of the bed, sideboard, or radio. When the furniture stores became frustrated with the lack of response to their letters, they sometimes sent a person out to try to get payment. Looking back on it now, I remember times that were hilarious. There was one occasion when a knock came to the door. We all went immediately silent. Of course the person outside would have heard us talking as he came up the stairs. And I am sure he didn't think a ghost switched off the radio. After a while my mother put her eye to the peep-hole, only to find herself staring into the eye of the person on the other side. On another occasion, my mother waited the usual few minutes for the person to go away, and we even heard him going back down the stairs. But this bill collector was more wily than the usual herd, because he must have crept back up. When my mother got down on all fours, to look under the gap beneath the door, she saw him on the other side—doing the same.

One Christmas when we, as children, still believed in Santa, on the morning of the big day, we were disappointed not to have anything. We had been looking at pictures of happy families, sitting around a huge food-laden table, the wrappings from their presents strewn on the floor. And here we were—sitting around our table, looking at the two plates there. On one was bread, and on the other a few slices of chicken and ham roll. We didn't go down to play on the road that morning. The other children would have their toys, and would want to know where ours were. So for part of the day we talked about what story we would tell the other kids—to explain why we hadn't brought our presents down.

There was a lot of demands on the funds of organisations like the St Vincent de Paul. Some years there were just too many people in need. They would have to ration their visits to a few weeks, and even then only to those who were literally starving. When the knock came to the door, usually on a Tuesday evening, there would be a scramble to hide any signs of apparent wealth. At one time, having a radio was considered a sign of prosperity, and this would be hidden, along with cigarettes, or anything else my mother thought might jeopardise our chances of getting the little brown envelope, containing one or two pounds.

One Christmas morning, though, I think I must have been about eight, I awoke to find our flat full of presents. These were second-hand, but that didn't matter so much. There were books, which I stored away for later. There were dolls, and wonderful toys which you could wind up with a little key on the side. We felt we were in an Aladdin's cave of delight. My mother filled the table with all manner of foods, some of which we had never tasted before. All this food came out of a large wicker basket, which we used as a doll's cot afterwards.

My sister kept talking about Santa, and how kind he was to us that Christmas. I kept silent. I had been there on Christmas Eve, when the presents came. I knew that our Santa was different than the usual picture we were used to seeing. Our Santa didn't have a white beard, nor was he dressed in red and white. He didn't come down the chimney either, but rather knocked on the door. He was wearing a suit, shirt and tie, and over this he had on a brown gabardine coat. He did have a helper with him though, and I thought he looked very like the St Vincent de Paul man who usually came on a Tuesday.

Joes Together

The seagulls woke me up, with their fussing and crying, on that Easter morning in 1959. Whenever we could, we would put out crusts of stale bread for the pigeons and gulls who were constant inhabitants of the high wall which was opposite to our back window. We had to stand guard over the food to make sure the pigeons got some, for if we didn't, the gulls would attack and frighten them away. It's not that we didn't want the gulls to get some too, it was just that they were greedy, and constantly hungry, and would leave nothing for the smaller birds. So we would hide behind the net curtains, so as not to frighten the pigeons or sparrows away, and would rap on the glass if we saw a gull hovering nearby.

Anyway, to get back to this Easter morning—the previous day my father had made a few bob from his car-parking duties on Cuffe Street. So we knew we would have food that day. To add to our good fortune, a client had given my father his old sports jacket. Of course, my father hardly ever got to keep any of these gifts, as we needed the money for food more than he needed to look smart. So around the corner to the Iveagh hostel he went, with the good tweed sports jacket. I think I remember he got five bob for it. We felt secure on that Easter Saturday, as we sat around the table, looking at the small pile of silver coins on it. My mother said this would do us for two days, and we never thought much beyond that.

'Well, we'll be all right for a couple of days anyway,' my mother said, 'though the pawn-office won't be open this Monday, so I suppose there'll be a big queue down there on Tuesday, and I'll have to get there early.'

'Will you not be worryin' about Tuesday, Cathy,' my father said, 'sure, haven't we got enough for now? You'll never guess who I had over in the car-park today.'

'Well, are you goin' to tell me or not?' My mother was never one for patience.

'Do you know the actor, Joe Lynch?' 'Of course I know him, do you think I'm an eejit or something?' 'Well, he parked his car with me today.' 'What's he like? Did he say anything?'

My father reached inside his jacket pocket, and, with a flourish, produced a ten-shilling note.

'He's a decent man, he's game ball all right, most of 'em give me a thruppence or a sixpence tip, but Joe Lynch gave me ten bob. Not only that, he stayed talking to me for a while, asked me how I was an' all. And do you know what he said to me when he was goin'? he said, "You're Joe from Dublin, and I'm Joe from Cork, and us Joe's will have to stick together.'. Do you credit that, Cathy? He treated me like I was the same as him, and I won't forget him for that.'

The next morning when I awoke it was to a strange sight. Standing on the window ledge were two large Easter eggs with a tiny yellow chick perched on top of each. My mother wasn't usually given to flamboyant

149

gestures but I wondered did she think we would believe these large eggs had come out of those tiny chicks? When I looked closer I saw two more eggs in boxes standing in the corner, complete with chicks. Were we now expected to believe that the chicks laid the eggs with boxes and all? It didn't matter anyway. The main thing was that we had two lovely eggs each.

The bells of St Patrick's and Christ Church rang out that Easter morning, but they didn't seem to have such a sad sound anymore. No, now they seemed to have a joyful note—they seemed to say that things weren't so bad after all.

There were previous Easters, when we had no eggs, and future ones, when we would have none either. But I'll always remember that particular Easter with fondness. Not only do I remember it because of the magical chicks, but because we, as children, had our faith in human nature restored. We had often witnessed our parents being treated as something less than human beings because of their poverty.

But Joe Lynch, a famous actor, had treated my father with decency, and he continued to do so over the years, when, every so often, he parked his car with my father. He didn't judge my father too harshly, when my dad had too much to drink, but treated him the same, maybe understanding that my father's life—being a semi-cripple and living in poverty—needed some release.

So thank you. Joe Lynch. Thank you for your kindness to my father—for the generous tips and clothes parcels, and for helping to make that Easter special for us. But most of all, thank you for your generosity of spirit, for treating my father like a human being, and bringing some joy into his life. Dear Joe Lynch, even though we've never met, I always think of you with fondness.

The Television Man

I remember the first television on our road. This was back in the late fifties, and although some parts of Ireland may have had television before this, it was a great novelty to us. A rumour went around like wildfire that a family living in the hall beside ours had a television. We gathered together and discussed whether this might be true. It was decided by the elder amongst us, Christy Dalton I think it was, who was all of nine years old, that we should go up to the family concerned—the Glennons—and ask to see it. There were about a dozen of us in the group by now, and we crept up the three flights of stairs to the Glennons' flat. Through a crack in the door we could see strange lights flashing and we pressed closer to try to see what was happening. Mrs Glennon of course heard us scuffling at the door and opened it about a foot wide to let us see. There it stood, this huge wooden box, with its flickering light and sound and its little screen. To us it seemed like magic! It didn't matter to us who was talking on it or what they were saying, it was thrilling. This 'show' went on for a couple of weeks until the Glennons got heartily sick of the crowd of children at their door.

Some time later, other families got a television set as well and it was less of a novelty than before. I was about thirteen when we got a television of our own. This was a huge box-like piece of furniture with a small black and white screen. Before that we had a radio which we rented for a shilling a week. The television stood resplendent on the sideboard just inside the door and it was just like a piece of furniture. It was polished just the same, and covered at night with a piece of cloth to keep the dust out. We only got RTE 1 on it if the wind was blowing in the right direction.

When the situation arose that there was a danger of being caught with no television licence, my mother shifted it to a position behind the door. I recall on a couple of occasions, my mother standing there telling the man that we didn't have a set, while behind the door Charles Mitchell could be heard reading the news. Be that as it may, my mother decided after this that we wouldn't rent a television, as she suspected that the licence people got the list of names from the television rental companies. So we bought, in about six or seven instalments, a second-hand set from a company based in Glasnevin. As this was a cash transaction, my mother reasoned that there shouldn't be any record of us having a television. To her way of thinking, she didn't see why we should have to pay a licence fee, it seemed to her that if television was there, it should be for free.

I can never think about those old box televisions without remembering the day when our set took flight. My father had returned home drunk, and my mother was, understandably upset because we didn't have enough money for food that day, never mind alcohol. If only my father didn't keep making excuses, maybe my mother wouldn't have got quite so angry.

'Ah, Cathy, I met me brother Frankie and he asked me in to the pub for a pint, I couldn't refuse him.'

'You couldn't refuse him, could ya not ya amadan, but ya could refuse to come home with the money couldn't ya?'

'I brought ya home some lovely meaty bones, I got above in the Iveagh Market, Cathy, ya see I was thinkin' about ya all the same.'

'And were ya thinkin' that it'll take three hours to boil them bones in order to eat them, ya gobshite?'

This went backwards and forwards for some time and my mother was getting more and more angry. During previous encounters, she had hurled cups and saucers, plates and assorted missiles at my father as he made his escape out the door and down the three flights of stairs to the street below. She must have been feeling more frustrated than usual because she looked around the room to see what object to hurl at my father this time. Nothing she saw seemed to satisfy her need to express her anger until her eye fell on the television set standing in all its glory on the side-board.

My father, experienced at reading the signs, had inched his way towards the door. It just goes to show the strength given to people when they are very angry because my mother was of a slight build. Nevertheless, she grasped the big box of a television, and running with it, hurled it down the stairs after my father. Luckily for him, it missed him by inches and went crashing down on the little landing below. A huge chunk of it was broken off and it lay there—beyond repair. It took two people to lift it back up and put it back on the side-board, where it had to be propped up on one side where the chunk was missing.

When my mother had calmed down she remembered that the television was still within its three-month guarantee period. The television man was called out to bring a replacement set. I'll always remember him standing there while my mother told him how it had mysteriously fallen off the side-board. He looked at the gap left by the missing piece and then he looked at my mother. He looked as if he was about to say something, but then seemed to change his mind. He contented himself with making a general observation while installing the new set.

'If I were you Missis, I'd move that television in farther on the table, you'd never know what could happen with people bangin' into it.'

'Oh, you're right there, sir, I'll move it in by the wall, so I will.'

We all had a good laugh when he had gone, as I'm sure he had too.

Tuggers and Toys for Rags

The rag and bone man had arrived on our road and there was great excitement among the children. He only came about three or four times a year and brought many shiny things. There were plastic windmills on sticks, little cars and trucks, and a variety of dolls and others cheap toys to lure the attention of the children. His horse stood patiently by while he did his business from the back of the cart.

'Toys for rags!' he shouted and it was like the Pied Piper of Hamlin had arrived as the children gathered round and stared wide-eyed at the display of goods. We all scattered and ran back into our flats to look for something to exchange for a toy. There was a fear that he might go if left waiting too long.

When I ran up to our flat my mother was keeping a wary eye on things as at other times I had taken good clothes and bedding in my eagerness to get a toy. I managed to get an old jumper which had shrunk in the wash, plus some old socks with holes in them. This didn't seem enough as other children who had bigger families had more to trade. I nervously watched his face as he examined my offering. The trouble with the rag and bone man though, was that he always seemed to have a derisory expression on his face so it was hard to know what he thought. He handed me a small plastic windmill on a stick. I was delighted with this as were the other children who got dolls or toy cars or trucks, but none lasted more than a day or two before falling apart. This didn't put us off however, as the next time he came around we were just as excited and willing to trade as before.

Granny Fitz, my father's mother, also dealt in old clothes and rags or 'tugs' as they were called. She was a 'tugger' all her life. She was part of a small army of women who went out collecting old clothes and rags to sell on. They would leave their homes early in the morning and scour the four corners of Dublin in search of a means to feed their families. The big houses in the suburbs were often a source of pickings as were the middle-class houses. They could be seen heading off pushing old prams in which to put their tugs. Sometimes they wouldn't have the full fare on the bus and would have to get off halfway to their destination and walk the rest of the way.

My Granny Fitz was one of these women, but she pushed a triangular wicker cart with metal wheels in which to collect her tugs. She was of an earlier era and walked the streets of Dublin in all weathers collecting old clothes. There were a lot of cobble stones on the roads then and the wheels of her cart sent sparks flying a she went along.

Some of the women dealt with Harry Siev in Meath Street. He would examine and sort the clothes and decide on a price. He was a rag and bone man and clothing merchant for many years. If there were any clothes in decent condition, the women might try to sell them to the dealers in the Iveagh Market on Francis Street.

Woolfsons was another merchant who dealt in old clothes and rags from the factory on New Bride Street, almost opposite the back gates of St Patrick's Park. Many local people were employed there, mostly girls who had left school at fourteen, which at that time was the legal age for leaving school. There was no free secondary education available then, and even if there was the girls came mainly from large families with low incomes and so knew their earnings would be needed at home. Their working day involved unpacking and sorting the clothes and rags and sorting them into separate piles to be baled up later. Some of the clothes were in dirty condition, indeed often infested with fleas and bugs. This was made worse in the summer, in the old factory building with poor ventilation, the sweating of the girls would attract more infestation. This coupled with the constant scratching, drawing blood, which in turn attracted even more unwanted attention from the insects.

I remember going up one day to see my sister Mary as she came out of Woolfson's after a days work. Mary at fourteen was two years older than me and I wanted to see the place where I might be working myself in a couple of years. A wave of girls emerged and I easily spotted my sister with her bright auburn hair. I noticed that the girls had little bits of paper stuck on their arms, legs and necks with spots of blood showing through. It reminded me of when my father shaved with a blunt razor and the cuts which he covered with bits of paper. I mentioned this to Mary and laughed. She didn't laugh but she looked embarrassed. I realised that I had been thoughtless and mumbled something in the way of an apology.

We went home and Mary washed herself at the sink. There were no baths or showers in the flats at that time. I remember thinking that I never wanted to work in a place where you would be eaten alive by fleas and bugs. I felt angry that my sister had to work in such conditions. People say that money isn't important, but it is if you haven't got any. I wonder did those people ever go for twenty four hours without food, not in a voluntary sense as in fasting but in a situation where there was insecurity about where the next days food was coming from. If they had that experience, then they might think that money was important all right.

When Granny Fitz died, there was no money to pay for the funeral. My mother and father went around cousins we hadn't seen in years to beg for money to cover the bare minimum of expenses. They managed to get just enough to pay for the coffin and habit. I can still see that plainest of coffins—relegated to a side altar at the back of the church. As far away from the main altar as you could get without being outside the church altogether.

The priest rushed in, looking for his money. On hearing there was none, he flung the holy water at the coffin, stormed up the church aisle, reefing on his vestments as he went.

We all knelt at the back of the church. We didn't feel worthy to sit near the front. The priest rattled through the Mass; there were no expressions of sympathy from him afterwards—just an angry look on his face. As a child, I got the message. I remember thinking 'If we had money we wouldn't be treated like that, even in death.'

Hot Spot

In his later years my father got the chance of a job with Dublin Corporation. I remember at the time there was consternation because at first, his birth certificate could not be found and he needed it to start work. It took a number of enquiries and visits to the Registrar's Office to finally locate it. This was my father's first official job and he looked forward to having a regular income but was also nervous at the thought of being supervised and the nature of the work.

His job description was 'Night-watchman for Dublin Corporation'. This involved sitting in front of a brazier of coals with a small open hut behind him. Often he would patrol the area with a lantern to make sure nobody fell into the hole he was guarding and which the Corporation workers had dug up earlier that day. This wasn't as easy as it sounds because in the darkness of winter and with the pubs emptying of drunks who went stumbling about, this required my father to act somewhat in the manner of a sheepdog—herding them away from the hole. Then there were the occasional gurriers who thought it funny to push each other towards the hole.

Things went great in our flat for a couple of weeks when my father came home on a Friday with his wages and as the saying goes we were 'on the pig's back', but then he started to slip back into his old ways of not coming back with the money until late when a good portion of it had been spent in the pub. This maddened my mother who had been looking forward to having regular money, maybe even buying a radio instead of having to rent one.

Because he worked late into the night, my father slept late in the day. Also he would be moved around so that when a hole had been filled in and smoothed over he might be sent to another location to guard another hole or an entrance to a premises which had been excavated by the Corpo. Sometimes he would be situated near a pub and be tempted to slip away for a couple of pints. He had just returned on just such an occasion and settled himself in front of the brazier when my mother caught up with him. He sat there, his overcoat pulled tightly around him, his cap tilted slightly over his eyes. He was startled to see her there in the darkness and from the look of her he knew it was not good news for him.

'There ya are, Joeboy, still guardin' your hole I see, afraid someone might run away with it are ya? Or God forbid that the Corpo might fill it in.'

Getting no response, she grew angrier. 'Speak up why don't ya, I bet ya have plenty to say to your cronies in the pub, that bunch of lousers.'

My father muttered something on the lines of maybe having ten shillings to give her. This maddened her further and with a scream she lunged and tipped the hot coals of the brazier onto his lap. It was his turn to scream now and he jumped up and danced about, and with the smell of scorched cloth in his nostrils, he ran down the street and around the corner, his trousers emitting a trail of smoke as he ran.

Sheep's Wool and Fishing Rods

In the early sixties I was attending Whitefriar Street Primary School. At that time you could legally leave school at fourteen. There was no hope for most of us for going further with our education as back then there was no free secondary education. I remember our class being brought around Jacob's biscuit factory and being told if we were very good we might get a job there. Being a pale, skinny anaemic child I wasn't looking forward to it. In fact I almost passed out with the heat in the factory. However Jacob's was considered to be a good steady job.

School for me was very boring as we were on the same English book for a year. I had long since learned off by heart 'Heaven Haven (a nun takes the veil) by Gerald Manly Hopkins, and 'The west wind' by I can't remember who. Anyway me and Bernie lied about our age during the summer holidays and got a job in Davies cap factory which was across the road from the school. Bernie was an epileptic and it was hard if you didn't know her to understand what she was saying. People said of her that she was a bit 'wantin' or a bit 'simple'. Bernie would take a fit sometimes if she got too excited, so we had to be careful about what films we went to see. There was one occasion though when she had a seizure in the foyer of the Tivoli before we even went into the cinema. Con, the usher knew what to do, and he placed her on her side and made sure her airways were not blocked and we waited till she came round. It was alarming to see her lying there, spasming and shaking. Then Bernie would have to go home to bed, sometimes for a couple of days. Back then there wasn't the medication available that there is now. Another time when this happened was on her First Holy Communion day. It had been raining earlier and the channels were running with mucky water. Of course Bernie was excited in her white dress and veil, and it had been a sacrifice, coming from a big family to provide these extras. As luck would have it, when the fit took her, she keeled over straight into the mucky channel. Her mother came running out and was very annoyed with her at having ruined her new clothes.

In Davies cap factory I was put to work stitching the men's caps. Unfortunately, Bernie was put on the big steam presser. The trouble was she kept forgetting to take her hand away when she brought the press down. No matter how many times she was shown, she just didn't understand about timing. On the second day the boss told her—'Go home now love, your mammy is lookin' for you'.

I left school soon after that and got the first of many jobs. In those days it was easy to get a job in a factory. You could leave a job on a Friday and start a new one on the following Monday. It was usual to work a back week which you got back if you gave a week's notice on leaving, so it would be the end of the second week before you would get any wages.

Of course, all these jobs were low paid. Some stood out because they were unusual. Some were memorable because of their unpleasant aspects, while others were so short lived, I can't even remember their names. All were low paid. The pay was from about thirty shillings to two pounds a week.

One of my first jobs was with a company which produced fishing rods. I had a short interview on a Tuesday and started work the following morning. The company was situated on the quay just before Capel Street Bridge. Anyway, I was put at a bench and got a ten-minute instruction on binding the handles of fishing rods. Various colours of binding wire were used for different parts of the handles. After a while, I realised I hadn't got a clue about what I was doing. Since the policy of the company was to give you a few minutes training and leave you to it, I carried on regardless.

Who knows how many fishermen stood on the banks of a river and cursed heartily as the binding came undone? There were different colour bindings and different notches on the handle and I felt like throwing them all out of the window. It felt like I was one of the fishes caught by the rods I was fumbling about with.

There was another place on the quay where my job was to sort out the knots in sheep's wool. This was untreated, unwashed sheep's wool. Of course, in those days—the early Sixties—no-one thought it was necessary to wear gloves or protective clothing. The workplace was situated in the upstairs of an old building and it was smelly and sweltering in the heat of summer. Part of the reason for the smell was the untreated wool. Also we were instructed to cut out the cacks—lumps of sheep shit—which the frightened sheep had left behind.

I was there one Monday afternoon when one of the girls went mad and started throwing the shit at the window. She was screaming 'We're all shite, we're all shite!' Of course, none of us was allowed to leave our workstations and we watched as she ran downstairs and bolted up the quay. The shit was left on the window until the weekend.

Another early job was in Tailor's Tobacco on Francis Street. A lot of the factory jobs I remember then seemed to be in ramshackle old buildings. I was shown into a large room, each side of which was lined with long old wooden tables. Two women were assigned to train me in—Effie and Emmie. They sat there clothed in navy overalls, both women with brown hair streaked with grey pulled back in buns. I wasn't trusted, at first, to weigh the plugs of tobacco on the brass scales. My job was to wrap and label. Effie and Emmie wielded their cutting knives with serious intent, placing each cut piece of tobacco on the scales with slow deliberation. After a while I felt like chewing the table.

Every morning Effie and Emmie talked about what

the cartoon characters Mutt and Jeff were up to in the previous day's newspaper. To hear them talking you'd think the characters were real people. They never seemed to go out anywhere and never talked about romantic matters. You got the feeling that maybe they were content with their lot or if they weren't, well, they would offer it up for the good of their souls. Sitting there quietly, my fourteen-year old self was screaming inside saying—'Why don't you two old bags shut up and stop yakkin' about Mutt and Jeff all day long?' Of course you wouldn't have known this looking at me, I tell you the inscrutable Orientals had nothing on me.

Another part of my job there was to be sent downstairs to the cigar room to learn how to roll cigars. This dimly lit room was presided over by the world-weary Fitzer who reigned over his domain with a quiet authority. He stood there, his arms folded, his white hair sticking up in unruly tufts. A man of few words, he mainly pointed at things and maybe let a word or two escape through his almost closed lips. All around the walls hung tobacco leaves of various hues and strengths. There were about six men and boys there and I was the only female. Strangely enough I never felt intimidated about this. The only apprehension I felt was about not being able to do the job properly.

Many times Fitzer showed me how to roll the leaves to make a good firm cigar. I'm afraid that my efforts were not going to be sent out to any important clients.

However, Fitzer never lacked patience with me and I emerged more knowledgeable about tobacco leaves but still lacking the skill to roll a good cigar.

Boileau & Boyd

Boileau & Boyd was a pharmaceutical and beauty products manufacturer. It was situated on Bride Street in an old building with many nooks and crannies, old wooden stairs, with large rooms on four levels. It was very handy for me to be working there at the age of fourteen and a half as it was only five minutes' walk from where I lived.

It was a great place to work in because it made so many different products, and this made the work, although mundane, at least varied. Also, the pay was a little better than the average at the time in the early Sixties. Boileau & Boyd was the only place I worked in where the girls were paid more than the boys. Usually the opposite was the case.

My first task there was working in the bath-cube room. Seated at a long wooden table along with about eight other girls, we wrapped and labelled the bath-cubes. At the end of the room was a large Victorian-looking machine which wheezed and rattled and belched out the bath-cubes.

Occasionally we would get browned off with the work and someone would chuck a stone or piece of wood into the machine. It rattled all the more and soon came to a stop. It was time then to send for Larry, the maintenance man. This gave us some entertainment as he strode in, clad in his brown coat, looking serious. We would giggle all the more. After some thumping and banging he would locate the cause of the trouble. We all kept our heads down and eyes averted as he slowly looked us over. After a couple of minutes he would leave, breathing heavily.

At a level below was the perfume and shampoo room. In large sinks we washed out the bottles for the shampoo and placed them in position for the machines to fill. The perfume was expensive—Charles of the Ritz was one of the products we packaged. Some of the perfume bottles were too small for the machine to fill, so then we filled syringes with the scented liquid and injected them into the bottles.

Another job was to weigh phenobarbitone tablets—500 at a time—and pack them into bottles and cartons. Then there was the false eyelash room. The girls working there seemed to consider themselves as a species apart from the rest of us and kept to themselves. Their supervisor was a very glamourous young woman. The girls in the eyelash room were not required to do any other work.

The hair removal room was a scene of much hilarity. Many were the jokes about hair and the lack of it. Of course, we were not sophisticated enough to make subtle remarks, the comments were of a ribald nature— 'Ah, in the bedroom, where there's hair there's comfort, where there's none there's a row.' On many occasions the hair removal machine became clotted with the cream and Larry had to be sent for. Larry was a stocky, swarthy sort of man, and even though he was born and bred in Dublin, he had a Latin look about him. The thing was, though, that Larry was very hairy, with the exception of his head, which was almost hairless. Of course this gave rise to the remark—'Eh, Larry, who dipped your head into the machine?

Swirls of black hair grew up his arms and onto his shoulders. Bunches of it could be seen trying to escape from his shirt front. Because he often had to climb up and put his arm up to the shoulder into the machine to unclog it, this resulted in one arm remaining very hairy, and the other becoming completely hairless. Of course this resulted in his nickname—'Hair today, gone tomorrow'.

Then there was the Rulene room. Rulene was a liquid produced for the scouring of pigs. Located at the basement level, it was mainly the lads who worked here. Sometimes, though, if a boy or girl were considered too unruly, Mr Kennedy, the manager, and Yvonne, the supervisor, would consult and decide to send such a one down to the Rulene room. This sentence was usually for a week or two to teach us a lesson. Mr Kennedy strode about in his white coat and hardly ever said anything except an occasional 'Harrumph'. I suspect he didn't know how to deal with us, and was of too kind a nature to 'deal' with us in the approved fashion.

On starting work in Boileau & Boyd you would be required to sign a form authorising a search of your person should management request it. I never knew of anyone being searched in the time I worked there. Of course, there were many temptations, what with the perfume and cosmetics. This became especially so near Christmas as at this time we produced beautiful gift sets. The management turned a blind eye and it was somehow understood that as long as we weren't too greedy, then nothing would happen.

The lax atmosphere, though, led some to become careless. One day Assumpta was sitting working at her bench, when Mr Kennedy strode by. A large bottle of lotion could be seen sticking out of her open bag. Of course, something so blatant could not be ignored and she was sacked on the spot. Her sister Julia outdid her, though. One warm summer's day, Julia was just about to leave the factory for home when a bottle of perfume concealed in her bra exploded from the heat. There was a kerfuffle and shaking as many tiny pieces of glass were trapped in her clothing and on her skin. She had to be taken to the first-aid room. After her minor cuts were taken care of, she was told not to bother coming back.

When I remember my time in Boileau & Boyd's I do so with a smile. It was a kindly place. Anyone I know who worked there likened it to a holiday camp, especially compared to some of the factories we worked in later.

Ever Ready

One of the factories I worked in was Ever Ready batteries in Portobello. It was necessary to undergo a medical examination by the company's doctor before starting work. This was fairly routine—breathing, blood pressure and flexibility.

It was a large factory employing men and women. On one wall was a large office with windows looking out on the factory floor. The white-coated managers sat there looking serious. Like a lot of places at the time, talking among the workers was discouraged. There were many long benches with various pieces of equipment used in the making of the battery cases—coils etc.

We developed a sort of radar as to when one of the managers looked up from his paperwork to survey the workers. Also we became skilled in a type of ventriquilism—talking out of the sides of our mouths. We were changed around a bit, everyone taking their turn on the machines which required only one person. One of these was an extruder machine. You would sit on a high wooden stool equipped with a long metal rod which had a hook on the end of it. The machine coughed out the metal battery cases into a wooden crate below. When the crate was full it was time to remove and stack it on top of the other full crates. The hooked rod would be used to remove any faulty cases and place them into a different crate. In the first couple of hours I managed to spot a few faulty cases but after a few hours of this the machine could be belching out cases shaped like Donald Duck for all I would have noticed.

There was another machine high up and accessed via a ladder-like stairs. This mind-numbing and lonely job required you to climb up and feed the cases into the hopper. You never knew, when going into work, that on that day you might be required to do this job. So it could happen that you would be wearing a short skirt. The lads would be staring, as lads do, and getting a right eyeful as you climbed up.

Another unusual feature of Ever Ready was the toilets. There were banks of toilets on either side of the room. In the middle of this was a box which resembled two bay windows stuck together. The bottom half was made of wood and the top was of glass. Perched inside was a white-haired, white-coated woman. Her job was to take note of the time we spent in the toilets. We were allowed three minutes. If you transgressed this rule there was a threat that you would be reported to the management and on the third offence there loomed the possibility that you would be sacked.

I have never before or since come across a factory with this surveillance in the toilets. Sometimes, though, when one of her cronies was in the toilets the supervisor would be distracted talking to them. We took advantage of this to hide behind a wall and have a chat and a fag. Usually the talk was about money worries or giving out about the job, but sometimes the subject turned to more personal matters. One of the women was worried about her boyfriend's lack of energy in general but particularly in the bedroom department. After some time listening and making sympathetic noises one of the women grew impatient with this.

'Why don't ya bring one of them big batteries home for him, maybe that'll get him goin', after all they're not called Ever Ready for nothin'.'

There was a shocked silence. We all looked at each other and then burst out laughing. Even the woman with the limp partner joined in.

Bird's

The next job I had after Ever Ready was in Bird's Jelly and Custard on Little Ship Street—though the factory entrance was located in Chancery Lane. I was only a month working there when I was hospitalised with acute appendicitis. The company paid me in full for the three weeks I was out. It was also arranged that I was not to be given any heavy lifting jobs for a while after returning to work. On starting back to work I was issued with a white double-breasted coat and cap. When I came in on the second day and went to my locker I discovered that my new white coat had been replaced by a worn one with most of the buttons missing. Looking round it was impossible to spot who had taken it—there were so many girls around.

Like every other factory I knew of, once somebody got married they had to leave. In Bird's there were many single women in their forties and fifties who seemed content to stay working there. So it was unusual then, to have a married, pregnant woman being allowed to return to work. To us, it seemed almost like getting a dispensation from the Pope.

We produced and packaged many sweet products such as Bird's jelly, custard, Angel Delight, trifle and many more. The only jelly flavours I had tasted at that time were strawberry and raspberry. I was surprised to find the jelly flavours we produced also included orange, blackcurrant, lime and greengage.

I remember there was a hullaballoo one day when by mistake the factory got delivery of the toilet rolls which were meant for the office staff. Of course this meant that they got the ones intended for the factory. Well, I'm not joking, you'd think there had been a diplomatic incident the way they went on. Until then we didn't know that the office staff's bums were softer than ours. Well, I suppose with names like Nollag and Erin it is understandable that they shouldn't have to put up with toilet paper of a coarser quality.

In any case, at some unknown time the toilet rolls were switched back and things settled down again. In such little ways did I learn about how the world works. Bird's was a good employer, though, and treated their staff well.

Spot Dog Food

As we entered the swinging sixties there were numerous articles in magazines and items on film and radio about Carnaby Street in London, Mary Quant, fashion icon and designer of the mini skirt, the Beatles, the Rolling Stones etc. But although we were enthralled by all this glamour, it was far removed from our teenaged lives. It was around this time that I got a job in the Spot Dog Food factory. This was next door to Keeve's the knacker's yard in an area known as Blackpitts. 'Knackers' was a term used to describe renderers of animal flesh. 'Knackered' was also descriptive of something that was 'done in', that had come to the end of its usefulness or working life. When I think about Blackpitts I remember the smell of the place. From streets away, you could find it just by following your nose. I don't know what the history of the area was in the nineteenth century, but when I was a child it was a place of death—animal death, that is. A whole industry had developed in the rendering and treatment of animal carcasses. I suppose the very name—Blackpitts—suggests some awful disposal area.

As you entered down the cobbles of the factory yard, on the left was a stall containing two or sometimes three horses. Sometimes I would be surprised to see a thoroughbred animal there—young and frisky—and guessed that it no longer won races or brought in profit for its owner. So here it was, ending up in the knacker's yard. This was in stark contrast to the usual animals corralled there—old worn-out horses. All, however, ended up in the tins of dog food.

There was one occasion when I arrived into work on a Monday morning to find a horse lying dead across the cobbles outside the stall. From the smell I guessed it had been lying there for a couple of days. I wondered how it had got outside the stall, and when I asked I was told that one of the other horses must have kicked it to death. There seemed to be no hurry to remove it and we had to step around it to get into work. All that day and for some time afterwards I worried about how the horse must have suffered. There was no question about asking anyone in authority about it. It was understood that you just kept your head down and said nothing.

I was lucky in a way, because I was put in the shed with three others. Our job was to stick the labels on the tins and put them in wire crates. One wall of the shed was open to the view across the yard where the butchering and processing of the meat took place. On a few occasions, I was sent over on some errand, but I was careful not to cross the threshold. I knew that those workers inside were waiting for an opportunity to 'break me in'—that is, smear bloody intestines across my head and face. This would cause them much hilarity and wasn't considered particularly cruel as they thought it a sort of initiation. However, I had seen others after such an experience and they had been shaken and upset. Others pretended it was all right, but I could see the dismay in their eyes.

Of course, with all this meat about, it got on our shoes and clothes and was tracked into the cloakrooms. I tried to get in early so that I could hang my coat on one of the higher hooks. This was because the floor, despite regular sweeping, had chandlers—large maggoty worms—slithering and crawling up the walls. None of us wanted to bring our work home with us in the form of maggots.

It is strange to think, or maybe not, that in most other factory jobs I worked in there was some enjoyment, some lifting of the mood due to humour and camaraderie. But looking back on this time I honestly cannot remember anything of that nature in Blackpitts. Maybe it was because the stench of death hung over it.

Aggie and Mags

They lived at the top of my road—these two sisters. They seemed old to me at the time, but I suppose they were only in their forties. Aggie, the older sister, and Mags the younger, avoided men as if they were the enemy, even men they had known as neighbours all their lives. Although Mags never got involved with men in a romantic sense, she liked to flirt a little and embarrass herself and everyone else by simpering at married men as well as single ones. Luckily for her none of her intended targets took her seriously. Everyone knew that she would run a mile if they did.

The sisters went around everywhere together. They looked a little odd with their old-fashioned clothes and their hair cropped to just below the ear with side partings. Also they smelled a bit and their fingernails looked dirty. They seemed unaware of this, however, for their eyes were set firmly on the next life. Haunting the church was their main pastime as well as collecting rosary beads. There was one time when someone gave them rosary beads which had been bought and blessed in Lourdes and their joy knew no bounds. The sisters seemed convinced that the beads had healing powers and pressed them on sick people together with a sprinkling of holy water. If the sick person subsequently died, they claimed the beads helped them to die in a state of grace.

There was one man Aggie and Mags tolerated in their lives and this was a man called Martin. Martin was a religious eunuch who worshipped at the feet of the Blessed Virgin Mary. His devotion was remarkable and it was said of him that he never knew a woman in the biblical sense, but then what mortal woman could possibly aspire to the standard of Blessed Mary Ever Virgin? Going to Mass every day and wielding the collection plate, his humility knew an inner pride in his holiness. It seemed unfair that ordinary Dubliners didn't appreciate his piety but rather made remarks like 'That oul' craw thumper, it's a pity he doesn't go off with himself and join the priests—maybe they wouldn't be able to put up with him either.'

Aggie and Mags loved going to funerals, even if they didn't know the person. There they would be—right up at the front of the church, their eyes watching the faces of the bereaved, drinking in their grief. They scanned the newspapers looking for reports of fatal accidents. They would be especially interested if the dead person was young, as this guaranteed a big turnout at the morgue and then at the church and graveyard. This meant they could be in the midst of the crowd and people assumed, because of their tearful eyes, that they were somehow connected to the dead.

Those who knew them, avoided them, even the priest sometimes, when he saw them coming, hid behind the door. On a Sunday morning as Aggie, Mags and Martin knelt in church people behind nudged each other. 'Eh, there they are 'atin' the altar rails, Holy knickers an' The Virgin Mary.'

'And do ya see who's with them as well? Martin, the creepin' Jaysus.'

'They wouldn't give ya a loaf of bread if you were dyin' of the hunger, but they'd rattle their rosary beads at ya all right.'

When my sister died there was another young girl at the morgue who had died as a result of falling under a bus as it pulled into the stop. The place was so packed with people that it overflowed outside. As my parents and me walked home after the funeral we spotted Aggie across the road—it was as if she had been watching out for us after the funeral. Her eager face shone with the excitement of a voyeur of death.

'Quick,' my mother said, 'quick before she collars us.'

We almost ran down the road to avoid contact with her, but Aggie was not about to be denied. She caught up with us just a few feet from the sanctuary of our hall door. My mother, who was usually able to hold her own, was drained from crying and grief and it was she Aggie zoned in on. She put her face close up to my mother's. 'How are ya? It was a lovely funeral wasn't it, but sure isn't she up there in heaven? Ah but she didn't last long. Poor Mary.'

My mother, who was trying not to cry in front of Aggie, not to give her the satisfaction, finally gave way.

Aggie, having got what she wanted, drank in the last drop of grief and retreated back across the road. As for us, we climbed the stairs to our flat, had a cup of tea, and even though it was only the afternoon, we went to bed.

My Sister Mary

As you walk up Patrick Street towards Christchurch Cathedral, the last turn left just before it brings you into Back Lane. The first building on the left is the St Vincent de Paul Night Shelter for Homeless Men—at least that is what it was called when I was young.

Further up the lane on the right is Tailors Hall, the oldest surviving Guild Hall in Dublin. It has stood there for over three hundred years. Tailors Hall was a meeting place for the Tailors Guild and other guilds. Over its long history it has been a barracks and a court house. But it is best known for meetings held there in 1792 organised by the Catholic Committee. These came to be known as the Back Lane Parliament.

At the end of the lane, on the opposite side was a brush factory, but before you came to it you passed Winstanley's shoe factory, that more recently housed Mother Redcaps Market. But back in the early Sixties it was Winstanley's, and I went there once for a job interview. I was interviewed by the manager, a clean cut, white-coated man. He spoke with an English accent and asked me about my date of birth, former jobs and so on. When he heard my name he asked me if I was related to a former employee. I told him she was my sister, and he said he hoped I would be a better worker than her.

I couldn't bring myself to tell him that she had died a couple of months previously, and that she had been sick while working for him. I couldn't tell him that she had gone to different hospitals, including the Dental Hospital, because her fine white teeth had started to fall out. It was only when we were in town one day and she collapsed that anyone took her seriously. She was brought to Dr Steevens' hospital where finally they performed a blood test. She was diagnosed with acute leukaemia. She had just six weeks to live.

But as I stood in front of the manager of Winstanley's, I couldn't say any of this. I wanted to defend my sister, but was afraid that if I started talking I would also start crying. He wasn't to know, I told myself. But I felt angry that he had brought my sister into the interview. None of my feelings must have shown on my face, because he gave me the job.

I started work the following Monday. Winstanley's made shoes for leading brands including Saxone and K Shoes. Some of the work involved polishing and cleaning the shoes before boxing them up ready for delivery. It was important that no trace of glue was left on the shoes. We also produced custom-made footwear. One of the jobs I did was to get the wrinkles out of the shoes. This was done with a small hand-held flame gun which was carefully played over the shoe. Care had to be taken to ensure that you didn't apply too much heat, as this would shrink the leather and spoil the footwear. It wasn't too difficult with some shoes, but there were special orders for the softer leather shoes, which had to be treated on the last. I would hold the gun further away from the shoe so as not to spoil and shrink the footwear. The shoes I remember most were the ladies' boots—button-up ones made of the softest leather. Concentration was needed here as there were more wrinkles in soft leather, so there was a fine line between getting the wrinkles out and holding the flame too long and ruining the order.

One day as I packed away the fine shoes and boots, I imagined the ladies that would wear them, imagined their lives and the places they frequented. To me at the time, the height of luxury was to stay in the Gresham Hotel or perhaps the Shelbourne. I could picture a lifestyle that involved dining out in fancy restaurants, visits to the theatre, the ballet and the opera. Then the picture changed and it was me who was doing these things—like Cinderella, I too could go to the ball. What must it be like, I thought, not to have to work in a facto-ry, to have soft hands with nails like those hand cream and nail polish advertisements. The women in those ads always looked perfect, about to go out somewhere glamorous and exciting.

I was brought back to earth with a bump, or should I say a bang—in all my day dreaming I had managed to elbow over a pile of shoe boxes to the floor. Ah well, I thought, back to reality. I thought of my sister who would never have the opportunity to see what life would bring. Never have the chance to use her bright mind, her outgoing personality and kind heart. I remembered the two of us singing and dreaming of becoming pop stars. She liked Cliff, and I liked Elvis. The year she died, her particular favourite song was Gerry and the Pacemakers singing 'You'll never walk alone'.

When I hear that song now, so many years later, on the radio, at a football match, I remember the two of us learning songs off the radio and from music sheets, singing away together for hours. I hold these memories as happy ones we shared—my big sister Mary and me.